a *ZIGZAG* mind

SONAL MANSINGH

INDIRA GANDHI NATIONAL CENTRE FOR THE ARTS

Vitasta

Published by
Renu Kaul Verma
Vitasta Publishing Pvt Ltd
4348/4C, Ansari Road, Daryaganj
New Delhi-110 002
info@vitastapublishing.com

ISBN: 978-81-988295-2-8

First Edition 2025
MRP ₹ 495

Typeset by Shubhpreet Kaur
Cover Design by Smriti Maheshwari
Printed by Vikas Computer and Printers, New Delhi

Contents

Foreword

Knowledge in India is the purest thing realised through the guru-shishya paramparaa as attested by the Mundaka Upanisad when it says:

तद्विज्ञानार्थं स गुरुमेवाभिगच्छेत् समित्पाणिः श्रोत्रियं ब्रह्मनिष्ठम् ।

Fostering the rich and diverse guru-shishya paramparaa of our country, the Indira Gandhi National Centre for the Arts (IGNCA) conceived an ambitious programme entitled Diksha. Diksha primarily aims to raise awareness and inculcate our young generation about the rich musical-cultural traditions of India by inviting renowned and celebrated artists at IGNCA to share their journey and vivid experiences.

It gives me immense pleasure to place the book, *A ZigZag Mind* authored by Dr Sonal Mansingh ji, a saadhaka, dancer and scholar par excellence—as a remarkable souvenir of guru-shishya paramparaa. The book narrates the 'splendid resolution' of a 'woman in dance,' whose commitment to explore the rhythm of life required the distinct expression of an invincible self. Her ultimate discovery of the divine soul unfolded in the artistic endeavours that primordially manifested the Supreme Being in dance creations and performative environments. Sketching down such a personality in words requires a complex unravelling of a relationship between the dancer and the dance. Her multilevel and multi-scalar engagement with portrayals on the stage illustrates an intricate dwelling of the past and the present. Embodying varying characters of epic stories, the intricacies of sequence in the performances divulge her continual practice, accomplishments, and imbibed emotions since childhood.

The unique and episodic collection of stories in the book portrays the life journey of an artist, Dr Sonal Mansingh, an exponent of India's classical dance tradition. *A ZigZag Mind* is her autobiographical testimony of an artist's life that recounts unique and priceless moments of self-revelation.

The book has been segmented into twenty-eight chapters in which the author exquisitely illustrates various themes ranging from 'Guru Shishya Paramparaa', 'Making of a Classical Dancer', 'Creativity in Dance', 'Why Life is Divine', 'Yamunaa-Witness to Krishna Lilaa', 'Sapta-nadi', 'Why I am Dwijaa', 'Raadha', 'Draupadi', 'When the Gods meet' to 'Ramayana as Narrated in *Ramcharit Manas* by Tulasidaasa'.

The book unfolds with an interesting narration of the author about her gurus Prof U S Krishna Rao, his wife Smt Chandrabhaga Devi, Mylapore Gauri Amma, Vempatti Chinna Satyam, Kelucharan Mahapatra, and many more from whom she learnt the multi-faceted art of dancing. Highlighting the role of guru in making a disciple she remembers its age-old metaphor which is that of the potter. The paradigm artist in Indic tradition is the potter (kumbhakaara) who does not make anything, rather he only makes to manifest things which were earlier unmanifested. On the contrary, in the West, the ideal of an artist is the carpenter who makes things. An artist in India is a saadhaka, a yogi, a bhakta and his art is yoga.

Based on her own experience, the author beautifully differentiates the three components, namely, naatya, nritya, and nritta. Naatya is based on rasa; nritya is based on bhaava (emotions); and nritta (dance) is based on taala or rhythm and laya (time). At sundown, the dance performed by Lord Shiva is a manifestation of ecstasy without any purpose. He performs dance being merged only in extreme delight as propounded in the Abhinavabhaarati.

भगवान् तु आनन्दनिर्भरतया क्रीडाशील: संध्यादौ नृत्यति।

In this context, Shiva is known as Nataraaja, the cosmic dancer. Here, the author reminds us of the prime importance of dance in our life and the only source of enlightenment.

Besides public triumphs in on-stage performances, the author describes her inner awakening and her victories over the self. She gives references to Sapta-nadi (the seven rivers), the source of life and the rhythm of which gave tremendous momentum to the cultural civilisations that prospered on their banks. While the characters of Raadhaa, Draupadi, and Krishna represent the philosophical contemplation of India, their enactment in the play is a source of her inner awakening. The author calls herself dwijaa as she rose above her mundane body and transcended her limitless passion for exploring new frontiers of Indian aesthetics despite her meeting severe accidents and physical challenges. She also presents a fascinating account of re-narration of our civilisational text *Ramcharit Manas* by Tulasidaasa in the sixteenth century and how she adapted some of its important episodes during stage performances. Summarising the journey of Sonal ji in a book or in any form is an uphill task, specially, when you know her closely or at least if you think that you know her closely, you get so mesmerised with her multidimensional personality that you get confused which one to choose or leave for depicting her entire personality. One gets to believe that such persons only take birth once in a while. It is not only her illustrious career as a classical dancer which attracts you, but her commitment, dedication and emotional expression about Bhaarata and Bhaaratiyataa which has the capacity to change your thoughts and perceptions. So many books and articles have been written and published on her and many of her biographies have stood out as bestsellers. Many writing legends have written about her, still they look incomplete. Even this book which is being attempted to portray Sonal Mansingh (by Sonal ji herself) through her thoughts, may not be in a position to present her life and works completely. So wide and vast is her panorama. This book is only an example of her versatility where she has portrayed her writing talent. On behalf of IGNCA, I sincerely appreciate and express my gratitude to Dr Sonal Mansingh ji for her perseverance, magnanimity and dedication towards Indian art and Indian culture. I hope the book will be received with great enthusiasm among the academic fraternity and art practitioners and other readers.

Sachchidanand Joshi
Member Secretary, IGNCA

Preface

Over the past decades, I have written articles, short pieces about ideas and thoughts as they appeared like wandering clouds lazily scanning my brain or whistled past like a bullet train. They needed to be shared because of the quirky nature of some, along with their unusual experiences or acute observations. I liked what I read; some from a particular period of time when I was busy travelling, a few others based on my dance choreographies and a few on my life's experiences.

Normally a mind does not think in a straight line; at least, mine never did. It has zigged and zagged like the toy train from Cuzco to Machhu-Pichhu in Peru. I thank the Indira Gandhi National Centre for the Arts (IGNCA) for first daring to print and publish these articles in book form. I thank the member-secretary, Dr Sachchidanand Joshi for reposing faith in my writings. My thanks are also due to Simran for painstakingly typing (I always write in longhand) out articles written on stray pieces of used envelopes (in that I am a Gandhian, recycling and reusing every kind of paper) and ferreting out images.

Dr Lokesh Chandra who has been my friend and guide since

long, wrote a poetic Prologue. Dear friend Prof Malashri Lal, Rumu to me, for going through the articles and writing a brave critique. I thank Gunjan Dwivedi for making original drawings for chapter nineteen, *Same Krishna, Differing Perceptions.* The cover painting is by the eminent artist Nupur Kundu who gave it to me with so much affection. Thank you Nupur.

My thanks to all the unwary readers in advance.

Dr Sonal Mansingh
New Delhi
1 September 2025

Prologue

Dance is integral to life, to love, to passion, to creation. The male bird of several species dances before the female to produce tumescence both in himself and in her. Whether in bird or in human, dance is instinctive—passion throbbing to enrich life. Over the years, Sonal has emerged from being a sensitive danseuse to the Goddess of Dance or Vajranrityaa. She embodies the dynamism of the divine in the world of form. In the word of Japanese esoteric texts, she is the absorption of divine powers into dance to remove the darkness of minds so that they attain 'the freedom to roam at will'. She is the renaissance of wonder, the re-awakening of life to see the dream of the Eternal in the flow of movement.

Sage Bharata endows the abhinaya of Sonal with the ecstasy of movement born of the rapture of unending creativity—follow me to the spring and find its secret. She has filled and continues to fill the heart of India with hymns that hum with the timeless. The imperishable melodies of the songful Jayadeva throb in the flit of the carefree joy of the feel of Sonal. The prima ballerina, Sonal, supple as leaping fire, subtle as incense, enfolds the cultural scene of India with fiery energy. She is the creator of Classical Odissi in the music of the eternal. The Lord of Dance, Nataraja, as manifestation of primal, rhythmic energy, dances the nadanta in the golden hall of Chidambaram to sustain the phenomenal world. So does Sonal capture the wild of the wordless, the wandering (caraiveti) that leaves twilight behind, in her sensitive presentation of the panchakanya wherein a whole social fabric overflows in the splendour of continuity of the body in joy.

I was thrilled to see Sonal dance the imagery of the Charya-giti, embracing it as 'the song of the mystic path'. The discursive thought trailing in robes, her necklaces symbolising the esoteric mantras in the imagery of Munidatta, her art arose to heights that kissed the divine Mount Sumeru.

Sonal matures and ripens the transcendent soul, like the Goddess Nairatma, the essence of vision. Her dance carries her esoteric message to the skies and it rains down on the fields of the mind to kiss the breath of humankind. She gives eternity to the cold and subtle smiling lips of the great siddha, Shabarapada, whose mind flows along the stream of her movement. Her dance sends the dew of heaven to the earth where the Siddha kneels in prayer in an attempt to sight virtue.

Shall eternity leave her shoes on the shores of time? No. This book is a long-awaited journey into Sonal's golden dream world seeking the vibrating rhythms of the Song of Govinda. Eternal time marauded by inevitable moments lives in her art to lead us to the lucent shores of life. Many springs, where you, Sonal, soar and dance joy into the veins of time.

Prof Lokesh Chandra
Former President, ICCR

Chapter 1

Guru-shishya Paramparaa

'Show me the difference between that monkey and you' said my Guru, Prof US Krishna Rao pointing the rhythm-beating short wooden stick Tattakazhi at me. One hot May afternoon in 1961, I am trying very hard to reproduce bhava, expressions of a young woman desperately in love. 'Try harder. Eyes softer. Bend your stupid head and look up from under the eyelashes at the form of Shiva. He stands in front of you. Don't frighten the poor God away.' I don't know whether to laugh or cry. Tears come easily. My face reflects a puzzled look. We have been working at polishing the centrepiece of Bharatanatyam repertory (margam), it is the most complete, complex and demanding piece of living art ever invented!

I have got the 35-minute framework of the Varnam firmly etched in my mind with all the Jathis, those complicated rhythmic patterns arranged like units of words in a paragraph and Swaras—complicated patterns of Raaga notation—and their corresponding movements. The body is ready and raring to dance. Even the text in Telugu with meanings of words and context is committed to my photographic memory. But what of my face which refuses to plead, yearn, and pine?

A teenager of today would find the situation funny and incredible as most of them have already experienced love, attraction, passion, obsession and other similar emotions, but here I stood immobile until jolted into action by my Guru. That one piercing, arrow-like glance from him changed my worldview and my practice of dance. That same tattakazhi also landed firmly on my drooping forearm and elbow or a not fully turned out knee. I followed Guru's instructions to the last word, made faces, raised and twitched eyebrows, fixed yearning glances at an angle. Mirror was my friend egging on to try once more.

Therefore, the ancients praised the Guru as a combination of attributes of the trinity: Brahma-Vishnu-Mahesh: Creator-Protector-Revealer. A potter is quite like the Guru as Brahma who takes a lump of clay, and moulds it after softening it with water. The seeker or student is the clay.

Then the potter is the Guru as Vishnu, who kneads it and places it on the wheel to give it the shape of a vessel, a pot, a container with empty space within.

The potter-Guru as Maheshwara (Shiva) then places the pot in the furnace to bake it, making it perfect through fire. The resultant container is now ready for pouring in knowledge.

This metaphor for the Guru takes us further into the realm of spiritual dimension as the verse compares Guru with the Unseen Intangible yet all-pervading ParaBrahm, which is ever present in the heart, mind and energy of the shishya, the disciple.

The journey from novitiate to Shishyatva is life-long. Physical discipline and moves can be mastered by continuous practice and concentration and can be learned easily today by watching YouTube videos or through Skype or Facetime calls. Even so, without the eagle-eyed supervision of the Guru, without the constant interplay of exhortation, exertion and exultation of

At the feet of Guru

passing yet another milestone in Guru's expectations, the disciple does not fully get the essence and experience of shishyatva or discipleship. This is the state of Humility and Receiving in which each glance, gesture and word of the Guru become drops of elixir, full of life-fulfilling knowledge.

The Guru-shishya Paramparaa or tradition is as old as life itself. There is always somebody to inspire us and guide us from the time we are born. Mother is considered the first Guru because her thoughts influence the unborn, moulding the baby's character even while still in the womb before birth. Father is the second Guru because he provides in every possible way for the welfare and growth of the child. Then, if one is lucky, the 'call' comes from the Guru whence the process of moulding, shaping and filling of knowledge begins. Therefore, the Guru is the third revered person after mother and father in the Sanatana tradition.

Kabir, the great fifteenth century mystic poet said, 'Going on pilgrimage yields one good result; meeting with saints, yields two, but meeting and being accepted by a Sadguru is the greatest good fortune.'

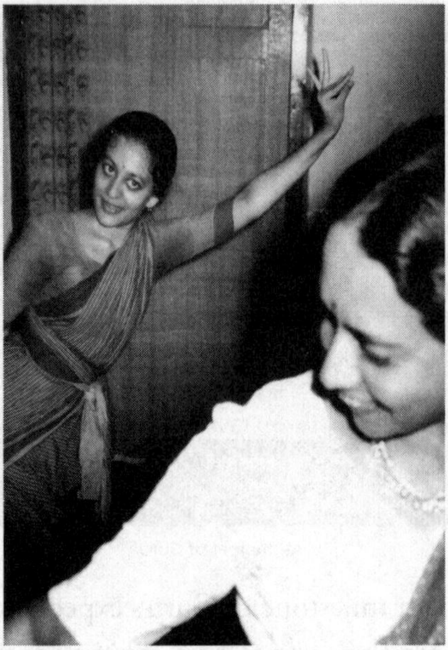

Learning by example from Guru
Smt Chandrabhaga Devi, Bangalore, Karnataka

I have been truly blessed to learn Bharatanatyam under Gurus such as Prof U S Krishna Rao and his wife Smt Chandrabhaga Devi who trained me in the pristine tradition of their legendary Guru Pandanallur Meenakshi Sundaram Pillai. I was also fortunate to have sat across the great Abhinaya queen, Mylapore Gauri Ammal who taught padams or songs replete with shringaarabhava, passionate love, without ever moving but with only her supple hands and intense expressions emanating from her one good eye!

My brief stint with Guru Vempatti Chinna Satyam in Madras to learn Kuchipudi was to understand Karanas of Naatya-Shastra and their practice in the three contiguous dance styles from Odisha, Andhra Pradesh and Tamil Nadu which gave me a fair idea of the cultural geography of India. Guru Kelucharan Mohapatra's kick on my bowed head proved to be a blessing that propelled me to explore uncharted territories of forgotten traditions and hidden treasures of Oriya literature, music and the performing arts. Further deepening of my search and expansion of frontiers happened with my decades-long association with Shri Jiwan Pani, poet-scholar from Orissa who became my friend, philosopher, guide and mentor. For my seminal work in Odissi dance, I earned the title 'Rukmini Devi of Odissi' in Madras, now Chennai. Rukmini Devi firmly re-established Bharatanatyam dance by exploring older traditions, building upon them and creating a well-balanced repertory. She is considered one of the greatest pioneers of dance in the twentieth century. Therefore, it was a great compliment to be called Rukmini Devi of Odissi by the dance fraternity and critics of Madras, a result of collaboration with Jiwanda (elder brother).

In the Upanishadic tradition shishya or the Jigyaasu i.e. seeker of knowledge asks questions to the Guru. In the ensuing dialogue, there is a lively give-and-take of ideas, with the shishya clearing doubts until the final and conclusive teaching from the Guru is received.

'Ask and thou shall know' is the principle which works

Gurukul-Explaining the Scriptures

alongside another equally significant principle: 'Ask with humility', never with attitude. During the 1980s and 1990s, we were able to ferret out gems from forgotten texts. For example, to answer my question about lack of mood music in the raagas or the classical melodic structures in Indian music—which are normally used to sing the Gita-Govinda of poet Jayadeva—the moot point is why those mentioned by him in the text were never heard; Jiwanda (da is short for dada or elder brother) referred to the compendium of music, Sangita-Ratnakara, authored in the thirteenth century by Sharanga Deva. From there, we found all the raagas mentioned in the Gita-Govinda, complete with dhyana-shloka or invocation of the mood of the raaga personified as a deity, man or woman, complete with scales or ascending and descending notes, jeeva-swara or the soul-note, and even the vaadi-samvaadi notes. Raagas such as Vasant, Maalav, Karnaat, Gujjari, Vaaradi, Desaakhya, Gunakri, and Ramakri, brought the text alive. Raadha's yearning, Krishna's entreaties, and the sakhi's (messenger / friend's) persuasion could be 'seen' and 'heard' in these melodies, Jayadeva received his due at last when we presented this Gita-Govinda in the National Museum theatre, a performance watched by the astonished cognoscenti of the dance, music and literary worlds.

At dinner in my rented flat in Defence Colony, Pt Ravi Shankar heard our researched work and exclaimed that he could recognize some of the raagas as the distant cousins of the now known Raagas but these were truly new and inspiring to the ears! Pandit ji's suggestions resulted in our first-of-its-kind seminar in 1983 where for two days, great scholars of music from the North, South and Orissa compared, contrasted and discussed these raagas. We had undisputed musicologists like Dr Sumati Mutatkar, music and literary scholars like Pt Dr Nilamadhab Panigrahi, Pt Markandeya Mahapatra and Pt Kashinath

Gurukul Activities (top); Vedic Ashram

Pujapanda, Shri Subrahmanyam and Smt Radha Krishnamurthy representing Carnatic music, and our own vocalist Pt Bankim Sethi who was coached in these raagas and asked to compose ashtapadis accordingly. There were music and dance critics who came to know and learn. Some among them later picked up enough material to write in their own columns.

Three vocalists from Hindustani, Carnatic and Odiya systems sat on stage and sang compositions with elaborations in two

Strict Guru

raagas: Vasant and Shri. These two raagas are commonly found in Hindustani and Carnatic systems of music, although these are sung with varying notations in these two traditions. Then, the first ashtapadi sung in Vasant from the definitive text on music, Sangita-Ratnakara, took away the collective breath of the informed audience for they could experience Spring! Similarly, Raag Shri gave a glorious new dimension to the known traditional renderings in Carnatic and Hindustani systems of music.

I can present scores of such acts of Guru-prasaad or benediction which I have received all through my life. In Japanese, the word for Guru is Sensei or Master. Just as a difference in levels of knowledge and authority is seen in these terms, student-disciple, every teacher is not a Guru, but every Guru is a teacher. Gurudom is not available in the market place. It is not conferred by the State or by kings. It is the state in which pure knowledge shines. The disciple drinks in the grace flowing from the Guru and gets enlightened. I rue the day when we began to hear and use words like ad-guru, food-guru, fashion-guru, etiquette-guru, techno-guru, IT-guru !

It remains to be seen if the Guru-Shishya paramparaa, a tradition in constant forward motion retains the core values or finally adapts to the easily available virtual world of the internet. Is this transition, transformation and transcendence even possible in today's world?

Chapter 2

The Making of a Classical Dancer

Tatt Tai Taam..,

Dhitt tai Taam...

Tai Ha Tai hi….. thus go the mnemonic syllables in the first, second and third speed played with the tattakazhi on a hard wooden block. This tattakazhi is also applied on loosely held elbows and lazy knees with equal abandon. The beat is picked up and produced by the dancer's clap-like sounds when the bare feet hit the floor. India's traditional dancers learn to perform on every surface—and this could be earth, wood, cement, marble or grass. A dancer first learns to produce flat-feet-claps, then, as feet, knees and thigh muscles become stronger, the arms join in. To arrive at the main ardha-mandali, the half-seated posture in Bharatanatyam, the back has to remain absolutely straight, elbows must be held up and stomach and bottom tucked in. To learn these elementary dance-units or adavus, the hands have to be trained to learn twenty-eight single hand gestures or asamyukta-hasta and twenty-four double hand gestures (Samyukta-hasta). These hand gestures are also known as hasta-mudra.

Geometry in Space

In addition, six (6) movements of the eyes and nine (9) movements of the neck have to be learnt to complete the design of each adavu. The simplest adavu in the Bharatanatyam style requires initial training of at least six (6) months of Yoga asanas and exercises to convince the Guru to begin on adavus, the basic units in dance. Both hands are placed on the hips as elbows carve triangles parallel to the knees, while both feet are placed in the toes out position. It is the first lesson in geometry in space created by the body.

As training progresses, other spatial designs emerge in circle, half-circle, perpendicular, square, and triangular formations. Sudden twists and turns, thrusts and leaps at three (3) levels—full standing, half-seated and seated on toes—take the student through the basic possibilities of adavus. Then, after perhaps two years, the first composition called Alarippu, 'the blossoming' is taken up. This brief dance makes a strong statement of the dancer's technical strength, understanding of the body in relation to space, and grasp of rhythmic structure. It is a warm-up for what will follow.

Nritta is understood as abstract movements of dance in which rhythmic cycles play a central role. The preparatory adavus, alarippu and jatiswaram are made of nritta sequences, belong to this element. The interplay of rhythm and movements spreading out in every direction in varying tempos and positions is a feat achieved seemingly easily but is attained after strenuous practice.

My Guru Prof U S Krishna Rao often quoted the example of three categories of students whom he described variously as stone, sieve and sponge.

Students who allowed teachings to flow away like water belong to the first category: Stone.

Those who retain only some part of the teachings are compared to a Sieve which allows rest of the content to flow away.

The best students are like a Sponge who absorb everything drop by drop and know when where and how to apply that knowledge.

Therefore, the ideal student is like the sponge who is transformed from discipleship into an ideal Seeker, thirsty for Knowledge.

'Discipleship' is the toughest state which can transform a person's body, mind and soul because it requires humility, trust,

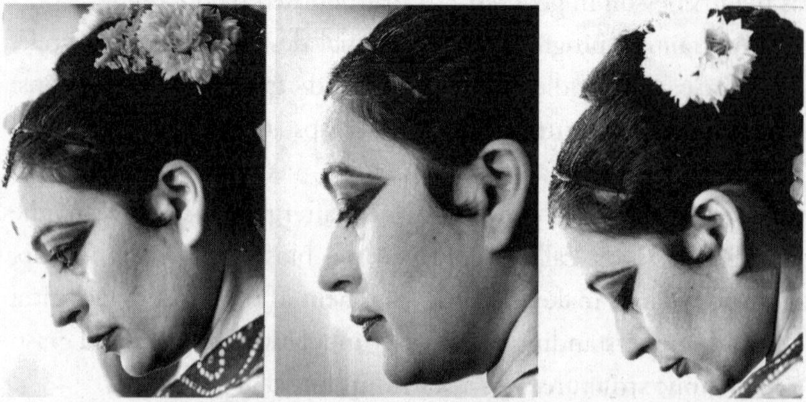

Meditation for Focused Energy

commitment and faith. It demands total dedication with laser-like focus on learning. It creates a strong mind in a strong body. It teaches us how to control and channelise emotions. It increases the power of concentration, application and observation. It teaches how any overspill of energy and emotion is to be saved, stored and used in a controlled and informed way for the purpose of creating aesthetic beauty. Exaggeration of any kind, especially in nritta compositions, may result in pulled ligaments, locked knees, frozen shoulder and even slip-disc. Dance is actually the ultimate yoga—dynamic yoga—and must follow the rules of a slow warm-up, regular and concentrated practice. I have been witness to well-known dancers in recent times undergoing knee surgery and treatment for slip-disc at a young age due to their misplaced enthusiasm or uncalled for leg extensions and jerky movements. Every movement must be well-calibrated and should have flow and logic.

The second element, nritya, is the real USP of India's traditional dance forms like Bharatanatyam and Odissi. There is a quantum leap from nritta to nritya which catapults dancer into a world of mystery, romance and every other imaginable emotion. Although nritya uses the same body language as in nritta, the dimensions are totally different. No emotion, mood or sentiment remains untouched as the dancer unfolds stories, situations and characters by using the very technique of nritta. Movement of eyes, eyebrows and neck is done with the purpose of enhancing a mood. Similarly, the vocabulary of hand gestures offers vast scope to infuse nuances in the depiction of different situations. The magic of applying the same hand gesture in different situations is unbelievable. A mudra to show digit '1' by raising the index finger can show '100' by placing it next to the eyes in which the eyeballs look like zeros. The same finger raised above the head would mean the 'ONE' or God.

Process of preparing for stage performance

The same finger on the lips would mean silence, but raised obliquely denotes threat. This mudra can also depict the world by moving in circular motions or even to deny or point a finger in accusation. There are more usages of this finger, but these examples should suffice to understand the depth and scope of the science of mudras. It depends on the dancer to use mudras judiciously not only to tell tales, but also to elevate the collective consciousness of the audience. Like a magician, the dancer creates an entire storyline teeming with characters with their individual mannerisms, characteristics, symbols and more, without support of any stage setting, props, change of costume or makeup. This is the technique developed in India for a solo dancer which is also what makes it so special.

Indeed for a solo dancer to hold the stage and the audience for recitals that stretch up to almost two hours is a feat unique in the world. This technique has been used in Bharatanatyam and Odissi at varying periods in history. I trained in this tradition from my early years both in Bharatanatyam and Odissi, learning this form of nritya through poetry and songs culled from the Rig Veda down to contemporary times. Understandably Nritya, also known as abhinaya, can be learnt from a Guru only up to a point after which the dancer charts her own path of interpreting the texts. The word 'abhinaya' can be interpreted as communication. It is made up of two words, the prefix 'abhi' meaning towards and 'naya', means to carry. Thus it means communication through dance in which the essence of stories and poetry is carried forward towards the audience.

In India, dances which are termed 'classical' are those that follow texts and compendiums like the Naatya-Shastra and other texts and commentaries. Whether solo, duet or dance-dramas, the Indian 'classical' dancer follows certain tenets which serve as beacons even today. For example, the five attributes of a good student-seeker are given:

- Be like a crow, who doesn't waste time in personal beautification/long showers, and in beauty parlours! It just descends in a puddle for brief moment to clean it's wings and claws, then flies away.
- Give total concentration on every word and teaching of the Guru just like the egret or crane standing on one leg to catch fish.
- Sleep light like a dog and be forever alert to Guru's call.
- Eat sparingly, enough to nourish the body.
- Be ready to give up the comforts of home and family in search of knowledge. Even Shri Ram and Shri Krishna went to Gurukuls to study.

काकस्नानं बकोध्यानं श्वाननिद्रा तथैव च।
अल्पाहारी गृहत्यागी विद्यार्थी पञ्चलक्षणम्॥

Even as dance skills of a solo dancer are counted as unique to India, what gives it further edge is the art of communication through interpreting life in all its dimensions of love, fury, wonder, mirth, pathos, heroism, fear and disgust. Solely by using the eyes, eyebrows, neck, hands and body held in certain recognizable postures, by varying gait and walk, the dancer draws characters on an invisible canvas and like a moving picture or a kaleidoscope, takes the audience on a journey of self-discovery. But every dancer worth her salt knows that the first appearance on stage is the alpha and omega of performance. Entry and exit are points that separate a good dancer from a mere performer or an amateur. There is no word for an amateur in either the much revered Naatya-Shastra or in any of the other texts and commentaries (point to be noted in these times of crowded social media platforms!).

A dancer is either good or bad. Performance is either gripping and leaves the indelible taste of ananda or bliss or it is eminently forgettable. Unlike in cinema and television, the dancer on stage does not get a second chance, and there are no possibilities of a retake! Neither is there any adjusting of camera angles or any time for throwing tantrums! Therefore, it is imperative to learn the ropes of being a good dancer early on in one's career.

Not much has been said about the need for every 'classical' dancer to be aware of personality traits and physical appearance, understanding of colours, make-up and costume. This applies particularly to the solo dancer. 'Less is More' is the catch phrase here and it aptly points to the need for paying attention to the axiom of Auchitya, meaning 'appropriateness'. Over-ornamentation, over-dressing, loud make-up, and too many colours, stripes and designs in costume obliterate, overshadow the dance as well as the dancer.

Those who understood the demands of building a career in dance made it through at times, uneven success graphs and yet attained heights of glory. They were those who lived and breathed dance at every step of their life which became a pilgrimage.

Female figurine of Mohenjo-daro, ancient civilization on River Sindhu

Chapter 3

Creativity in Dance

Why is it that each time I see the Sun set, I see new sights, new colours and new patterns. As I write this, greyish clouds have covered the Sun but the golden aura has created a proverbial 'golden lining', a few rays have escaped through the grey clouds and are illuminating the tall dark green Peepul tree and red-tiled roof of a distant house. Even as I finish writing these sentences, the kaleidoscope of the sun-cloud configuration has undergone four changes, each more enchanting than the other. Through a small window in the clouds, the sun finally peeps out, a naughty smiling face in full glory on the western horizon, an hour before setting. The clouds have lost their threatening grey and are pale in serrated ranks like defeated soldiers. The deep orange of silk cotton flowers, the last of the season, are happy to reveal their full glory, and a bow-like curved branch of the bougainvillea with its orange flame-like flowers competes for attention with those silk-cotton Shimuli flowers.

The clouds have formed a horseshoe around the sun as if in an attempt to mollify and placate as if acknowledging their mistake in trying to surround and subjugate the glorious Sun, the lover and giver of life. The earth is the beloved who has to receive his warm embrace and clouds, the jealous suitor who tries to stop that embrace. My mind captures these moments of yearning and struggle and rejoices at the victorious Sun smiling down at his beloved, the fecund earth. Love is everywhere. Love is overpowering. Love is triumphant.

How would an Indian classical dancer paint these colours and moods? She does not have the use of canvas, paper, paints and brushes like a painter, nor does she have the facility to write on paper like a poet or author. The stage is her canvas and she creates dark and light of shaded colours by her face, body and movements. With a flick of the index finder, she dismisses the errant lover or summons him before her. The same finger pointing upwards above the head offers the greatest philosophical symbol of the One, the Supreme Being. Placed near the temple and twirled around, it shows delusion, madness or forgetfulness. It is said that even while sitting on stage, the entire Ramayana can be depicted by a solo dancer using the language of hand gestures, movements of eyes, eyebrows and neck. For that matter, any story, episode or character can be depicted without fuss, frills and fanfare simply by learning to use the elements of Abhinaya, one's own body supplying the necessary tools of expression.

I have already sketched outlines of Nritta or abstraction in dance. Let me now give you a glimpse of the inner world and soul of dance. This is the element which links deep philosophical insights of life with literature, music and dance.

Any civilisation which has survived centuries of interaction with people who came as invaders, travellers, merchants or monks has many complexities and layers of different contexts. In India, the art of dancing existed from ancient times. The bronze figurine of Mohenjo-daro is arguably that of a dancer, standing in what is known as the Abhanga posture with one hand on a flexed hip.

Spontaneous Emotions of Naayika

References to dance abound in the earliest literary texts such as the Rig Veda and every subsequent text from Vedic times. Kings and queens were given training in dance and music along with martial arts. People danced in joy and in grief, at marriage, birth and death. Seasonal changes were greeted with dancing as were full-moon nights and the transition of the sun from the southern to the northern hemisphere. Sowing and harvesting brought young hearts closer and many stories were woven around courting, wooing and elopement. Rich or poor, old or young, rural or urban, the heart was all that mattered. It is this element which creates the magic and mystique of dance, pumping passion and power into life.

Creativity pertains to the mind and it is imagination that moulds action. In dance, creativity pertains to body or physicality of form and to content provided by the mind. If the mind is allowed to play in the field of mentally created visual images, (surely this must have been the origin of cyber and virtual reality of the Internet) a whole new world of transformatory images opens up. Mundane activities of daily living begin to acquire new meaning. Even actions like drinking water or preparing paan (betel leaf) can acquire special meaning when presented on stage in a dance composition. Such actions acquire further beauty and gravitas when a simple action of drinking water translates into a bee sucking nectar from a flower. Another transformation of this image could be in the form of a lover's kiss delineated through hand gestures and a rapturous expression on the face.

Indian classical dance believes in transforming reality with the body and face becoming instruments of nuanced expression. Stories and legends, myths and characters acquire more dimensions than originally intended. Krishna's battle with many Asuras or anti-Gods appearing in different forms such as

Dhenukasur, the wild calf, or as Aghaasur, the diabolical serpent, or as Trinaasur, the wild storm created by needle-like sharp grass, or perhaps as Putana, the demoness with poisoned breasts could, at one level, be a warning not to take anything or anybody at face value, while assuring that 'Evil' can be handled firmly and thus, be defeated.

References to pollution of rivers and bringing ecological balance can be found in episodes of vanquishing the poisonous Cobra-King, Kaaliya and in the lifting of Mount Govardhana, in *Srimadbhagavat*. Then again, the physical forms of Krishna and his beloved Raadha have filled the mind space of generations. Krishna's blue colour symbolises space while his bright yellow dhoti, the lower garment, shines like lightening in the dark clouds. The Rig Veda describes this yellow garment of Vishnu as woven from rays of the Sun! Raadha's fairness is like the moonbeam.... 'Raadha became a moonbeam herself as she sets out on a moonlit night to meet Krishna, the dark lover', wrote Guru Gobind Singh! The love of Raadha and Krishna with its million hues of concomitant moods is the stuff of pan-Indian philosophical, cultural and art traditions. A galaxy of characters from our epics, Upanishads, Vedas and Puranas, plays and poems written by Kalidasa, Bhavabhuti, Bhasa, including contemporary poets in languages as diverse as Sanskrit, Tamil, Telugu, Bengali, Odiya, Brij, Malayalam, Kannada, Gujarati, Marathi, among others, paint stories about gods and goddesses, kings and queens, warriors and priests, tribes and clans, presenting them to their audience through the canvas of dance.

Stories, whether imagined or from real life, which tackle relevant socio-economic-political concerns have been important ingredients of dance in India. Instead of pontificating from a political pulpit or taking an aggressive stance on the street, dance cushions such issues effectively by clothing them in an aesthetic garb which nonetheless hits the target, pulls at our heart-strings, and brings with them, a sting of unshed tears. I have experienced this in Pnom-Penh, Cambodia, in 1983. On the last leg of my South-East Asia dance tour, I had the satisfaction of visiting Angkor-Wat after a rather nightmarish visit to the infamous Interrogation Centre of the Khmer Rouge regime's blood-thirsty regime. Angkor smiled benignly even as I accidentally stumbled on a divine head rolling in the tall grass while I walked in its corridors, climbed up to the shrines on their high platforms and gazed at dancing apsaras, those heavenly nymphs with their bewitching smiles. I joked with the monkey-gods and greeted the guardians of the eight directions seated in nooks and crevices.

My two performances were presented at the National Theatre in Phnom-Penh. Before leaving back for India via Vietnam on the last morning, my group of eight (8) musicians and I were invited to visit the Royal Palace Museum in which thousands of silver, gold, diamond, sapphire and emerald Buddhas sat in deep meditation, untouched by glory or tragedy. Our visit concluded in a beautiful terrace-pavilion with mosaic floors and soft breeze wafting in from the Mekong River where we were to witness some Cambodian dances. About eighty young girls and boys danced and chanted verses accompanied by hand gestures and body positions similar to the training received by Indian dance students.

Teenage girls in coarse pink short dhotis held up by an aluminium belt, teamed up with a white knotted blouse, with their hair done up in a tight bun danced the Apsara dance. Beatific smiles adorned their innocent faces. Young boys in frayed trousers and shirts did the monkey dance with joyous abandon. Watching them, I experienced Ananda, supreme Bliss. The moment, however, was rudely disturbed by the tall, dignified bespectacled man—director of the Royal Kampuchean Ballet — when he ushered in a woman and two men introducing them as revered teachers of the Royal Campuchean Ballet. He simply said, 'They are the three remaining of a hundred who were here,'. Even before I could digest the harsh significance of those words, he spoke again pointing to the quiet group of young dancers— 'Each one is an orphan'. Waves of shock, grief and surprise hit me as my mind juxtaposed brutal images of the Interrogation Centre, the horrific tortures and skull-pyramids with the magic and beauty created by the dancers who may have witnessed the death of their parents in unimaginably cruel ways and had yet transformed those emotions through dance. The angst and sorrow of their lives were transcended and transformed through dance. This was the ultimate yoga.

We bowed deeply to this group of Yogis and humbly presented a purse with all our unspent money. I hold those moments close to my heart and have drawn inspiration in dealing with crisis situations in my life. The Ultimate Transformer is therefor Nritya-Yoga. Dance is the Supreme Yoga, the dynamic yoga which leads one to the Shoonya, the calm point of Being.

Chapter 4

Dance of Shiva

The Mirror of Life

'We should consider every day lost on which we have not danced at least once,' said Friedrich Wilhelm Nietzsche. Did he really also dance? I very much doubt, yet many great scientists, astronomers, geologists and mathematicians have been known to indulge in artistic activities like painting, playing the piano, violin, tabla and sitar. Somehow, these hobbies seem to balance the yin and yang energies. But Nietzsche goes a step further by declaring dance to be the raison d'etre—giving meaning to life.

I mulled over this quote for a long time. It is a profound statement, undoubtedly. Nietzsche's declaration confirms the verse from the more than two-thousand-year-old text—the Naatya-Shastra—purportedly written by sage Bharata, which affirms the prime position of dance in life.

न तज्ज्ञानं न तच्छिल्पं न सा विद्या न सा कला ।
नासौ योगो न तत्कर्म नाट्येऽस्मिन्यन्न दृश्यते ॥

There is no form of knowledge nor plastic arts like sculptures, no realisation of higher philosophy, nor any form of art, no

Nataraja

discipline of Yoga nor any other action on earth which is not seen in the complex art of Naatya: dance as a unit of music and acting.

Simply put, there are no arts, sciences, academic disciplines or situations which are not mirrored in dance! Dance is the container of life. It creates life, looks at life, addresses life, supports life and infuses it with love. From mini to mega, from here to infinity, from zero to numberless numbers, all these concepts can be shown and contained in a few movements and moments in dance. Felt at a physical level, the continuous dance of breath: inhalation and exhalation and the constant circular movement of blood coursing through the veins is indeed a manifestation of dance that is the ever-present, dance within our own body. Ancient civilisations have believed in the therapeutic and balancing benefits of dance because when physical elements are in balance, the mind too is calm and equanimous, faculties are sharpened and one gets clearer perception of the seen

Nataraja–Abhaya assuring protection. Dola Pointing downwards to uplifted left leg

Nataraja–Agni bringing light destroying darkness of ignorance

Nataraja–Damru creating sound vibrations Naad

and unseen, heard and unheard. Therefore, dance is seen as the highest form of Yoga.

Nritya Yoga occupies a place of honour and distinction in India and the great God Shiva has been given the title of Nataraja, King of Dancers. The image of Nataraja has occupied such a central place in arts and sciences that it is now measured scientifically to create and understand the graph and tangents of energy and balance. It was no surprise that India presented a beautiful bronze-cast Nataraja figure to CERN, located near Geneva, the world-famous European Organization for Nuclear Research on 18 June 2004, where it has a place of honour. As many physicists saw, rather perceived and comprehended, it was the image of the Shiva Nataraja which held the secret of creation and cosmic order, the reason, no doubt for Fritjof Capra, the Australian-American physicist to use the image on the cover of his famous book, The Tao of Physics. The diagram of Shiva Nataraja on the book's cover depicts the perfect Mandala,

Nataraja: Trinetra (the third eye) in the centre of forehead.

themovement of subatomic particles in constant motion in space.

If we seek answers to the many contradictions and complexities in life, then we only have to look at Shiva Nataraja for the key to resolve them. Water douses fire, yet the fiery third eye of Shiva Nataraja blazes undeterred by the gushing waters of the river Gangaa from the matted hair on Shiva's head. In this four-armed image:

- The left upper arm holds Fire अग्नि symbolising destruction of avidya or darkness of ignorance, hence it is a manifestation of vidya, the light of knowledge.
- The context of the left lower arm thrown across the torso where the fingers point downward at a gnarled figure with an ugly face gazing up at Nataraja's calm smiling face.
- The right upper arm holds a damaru, a small cylindrical drum symbolising the first sound, first vibrations, Naada-Brahm.
- The right lower arm is held in Abhaya mudra which means 'Fear Not', is also seen as benediction.

- Nataraja is perfectly balanced on the right leg with bent turned out knee, while the left leg is held aloft across the right leg as the left knee forms a gentle triangular shape. The torso is erect and shoulders are in a straight line. The gentle twist of the torso happens at waist level. The rippling muscles on the thighs and calves subtly indicate the erect spine in which the Kundalini, the life force that lies coiled at the base of the spine, is fully awake and is playing its cosmic role.
- This figure is crouched beneath Shiva's right foot which is firmly placed on the figure's spine! He is known as Apasmaara, symbolizing avidya or ignorance. This denotes stupidity, sloth, insolence, arrogance and intemperate indulgence which are indicative of a deep-seated aeonic ignorance about the true nature of Creation.

The balancing elements in the Nataraja image tell us that even if life is full of imbalances and contradictions, even as every

Apasmaara Purush- Symbol of Ignorance

situation has two sides, and every relationship also has a flip side at every level of existence, we traverse a zigzag path through which balance can be sought. So, if Shiva's third eye (the Agya Chakra, mystical centre of consciousness) can burn Kamadeva to ashes by the fire of anger, the smiling, cool moonshine emanating from the Moon on the forehead, calms those flames aided by the cooling flow of the river we call Gangaa, which is also the river of life. Gangaa is the perennial life-force in constant movement of nourishing life across time and space. Water has many synonyms in Sanskrit, with one of them being 'Jeevan', literally meaning Life. The river flows out from the Jata, the matted hair of Shiva symbolising dense vegetation of Himalayan forests.

The serpents coiled around his blue neck and on his arms, ears and ankles symbolise life itself. It is the renewing force as serpents shed their skin many times in a lifetime. It is also used as a metaphor for non-attachment, a state of shedding all that is extra or superfluous, the unnecessary baggage that we seem to accumulate in life. *Shiva Purana* narrates the episodes of Gods and anti-Gods vigorously churning the Milky Ocean to acquire the elixir of immortality, Amrit. One by one 12 wondrous, beautiful things emerge, such as:

- Wish-fulfilling cow Kamadhenu
- Wish-fulfilling tree Paarijaat
- Beautiful dancers Tilottama, Rambha and Urvashi
- The Moon (Chandra)
- The Conch (Shankha)
- Great elephant Airawat
- The fastest horse Ucchisravas
- Divine doctor Dhanvantari
- The lustrous jewel Kaustubh
- The garland of victory Vyjayanti

- Shree the goddess of wealth and prosperity
- The great bow Sharang

Gods and anti-gods put in more effort at churning but now it was their turn to shout for help as deadly poisonous clouds of fumes rose from the ocean. Cosmic negativity and toxic vapours coagulated as Halahala would not only put an end to their efforts but also spell doom for the entirety of Creation.

Their collective prayers reached Shiva who was meditating. He came on the scene and effortlessly drank the poison. By the intervening hand of his wife, Goddess Paarvati, the poison was contained in Shiva's throat at the Vishuddhi Chakra and his throat became blue, the colour of poison. Hence the epithet Neelakantha, 'he who has blue throat' was added to his name. When one can reach the stage of accepting negativity and jealousies which are around us, but are not allowed to enter our bloodstream, and if one can contain them by controlling the mind, one can approximate that yogic state of Ananda or Bliss.

This is what a dancer attains during a performance, yet the real test is faced off-stage when harsh realities of life can overwhelm the performer. This is the moment to imagine Shiva's blue throat and emulate the supreme example of transcendence.

Nataraja's matted hair is shown flying out in all directions like his garments, in contrast to the equipoise of his body. In a whirl of constant movement, is there always a calm, silent centre? The symbolism will remain incomplete without introducing the Dance of Devi:

She the Shakti; the Power making Him Dance
She the Master of both Tandava and Laasya
She the Other who watches as Shiva dances

These lines poured out from me when I sat intoxicated with Ananda. The cosmic energy and power to create and enmesh together as the Female and Male principles of Creation, maintains the balance and Dharma or the cosmic order. This is the true 'Mirror of Life' as seen and experienced by us mortals, if we are lucky.

Chapter 5

Secularism in Indian Performing Arts

The best definition of 'secularism' is to be found in the performing arts of Bharat. The word has acquired many hues of meanings and interpretations in the past decades in this strange land called India. From the dust of this vast subcontinent have risen diverse streams of philosophy which are now called religion! As long as those were understood and practiced as signposts for life-enhancement, there was harmony and balance amongst people. Daily chores were made interesting and rewarding by rituals and the practice of charity. Etiquette and good manners became necessary to maintain those invisible threads which bind people together. Collective celebration of the life-cycles of birth, coming-of-age, marriage and death bonded people even closer. 'Sharing and caring' became key for a society, for a civilisation which began boasting of booming agriculture and trade across the seven seas.

Five millennia ago, the Phoenicians and many others came to India by land and sea routes to trade and do business, and in that process of give and take, they left indelible marks of their traditions and culture in the new land. The Silk Route acquired

When the Gods Meet: Indo-Greek legends

special significance because of the strong impact on customs, concepts and traditions in large parts of India. In return, faraway lands acquired impressions and practices of Indian traders as far as Peru in South America, South and South-East Asia, and of course, in Central Asia.

Waves of travellers came from distant lands as explorers, preachers, pilgrims and traders, and increasingly also as invaders to this prosperous land. Their aim was to conquer, to rule and to establish separate codes and rules of governance, and soon their social and religious interaction and practices also left a deep impact. India became a melting pot of ideas. Religious practices found significant place in the daily lives of people and several social and religious movements sprouted all over from north to south and in the far-west. If Buddhism cut across the Himalayas to take root in Tibet, China, Japan and all of South-East Asia, it also went westwards up to Central Asia. Indic traditions pre-dating Buddha had already taken hold in South-East and south Asian lands.

The happy amalgam these early travellers left behind is for everyone to see even today. Jainism had spread across vast tracts of the Indian subcontinent before Buddhism and parallel to what is known today as Sanatana Dharma—the oldest philosophy of striving to know what is eternal and true in the nature of Creation. Thus the six 'religions': Sanatana Dharma (Eternal path) now called Hinduism, Jainism, Buddhism, Christianity, Islam and the late entrant, Sikhism, emerged as front-runners in India. Historians are still trying to decode the ancient civilisations at Mohenjo-daro and Harappa and those found in Gujarat and Rajasthan, while glimpses of existent customs and beliefs can be imagined from seals, pottery, and jewellery excavated from archaeological sites. I mention this as relevant to our theme of dance and music as they are essential for a healthy and harmonious society. We have already spoken about the majestic bronze statuette of a female dancer from Mohenjo-daro.

To appreciate the importance of the role of performing arts in contemporary India, one has to go back in history and therefore, understand the centrality of the logic of love and respect for each other's beliefs. The kind of supple catholicity displayed effortlessly in the performing arts remains to be truly understood and appreciated. There are many number of instances of Hindu musicians singing ghazals, shayari and sufi. I too have danced to texts from Bulle Shah, Guru Nanak Dev and Guru Gobind Singh, and have performed Jain prayers to Parshvanath, Bahubali and Padmavati, besides stories narrating the life of Amrapali from the Buddhist lore and parables on life of Mary Magdalene from the Christian tradition.

Muslim musicians regularly invoke the primal sound Aum and render compositions of Hindu saints and poets, shabads of Sikh Gurus, prayers and texts of Jain and Buddhist monks, besides prayers and hymns of Christians. Some popular examples are those of the Shaivite saint Lalleshwari of thirteenth century Kashmir who was also revered as Lalded by the Muslims, and

Nawab Wajid Ali Shah of Avadh (1847-1856 A.D.) who danced and sang dressed as Shri Krishna on songs he himself composed. The list is endless.

Let me share a couple of my own experiences. In 1979, I was dancing at the Internacional Cervantino festival in the city of Guanajuato in Mexico. I was then solo dancer with a group of eight (8) musicians for Bharatanatyam and Odissi. Earlier, I had choreographed a famous poem by the great poet Vallathol Narayana Menon of Kerala called Magdalena Mariam. The text in Malayalam was strung to Carnatic Raagas and was danced in the Bharatanatyam style. It describes the peerless beauty of Mary, her change of heart at the sight of Jesus and her surrender at his feet. The description of her copious tears bathing Jesus' feet, wiping them with her long silken hair, anointing them with perfume and kissing them was sung in a soulful voice. It was an open-air, huge arena with amphitheatre style seating for almost

Mary Magdalene

5,000 people and a stage that was half the size of a football field.

Concluding my two-and-a-half-hour recital with a joyous Tillana after the sombre Magdalana Mariyam, I was inundated with felicitations. Long queues formed to greet me and some Mexican peasants wearing Sombrero hats also came forward. With tears in their eyes and garlic on their breath, they sat down on their knees to kiss my hands. One of the organisers mentioned that they were among those in the audience who were loud in their cat calls and whispers early in the programme. But as they watched, and by the time Mary was danced, they fell to their knees sobbing!

Similar incidents have occurred in several places in India and abroad with Christian, Jain, Buddhist and Sufi compositions in my recitals. Another example is when His Holiness the Dalai Lama invited me to dance at McLeod Ganj's Tibetan Institute of Performing Arts four decades ago in Dharamshala. It was the evening of Baisakhi Purnima, a day most auspicious for Buddhists because Siddhartha Gautama was born, sought Bodhi-gyaan and attained Nirvana on this day. Watching my specially prepared compositions on Chariyageeti, especially Sabari, he doubled up

Shoonya mahari (Chariya-Geei), Buddhist Tantric Song

A sacred moment: arm-in-arm with HH Dalai Lama

in his seat. At the end, when he came on stage to greet and bless us, he said in a choked voice 'how did you know Sabari is my Kula Devi?' That voice has not left me yet.

Going back even earlier, on a typical afternoon while I was studying in Elphinstone College, Bombay, I would be greeted by Ustad Moinuddin Dagar and his beautiful wife Suraiya chatting in our home with my grandfather. They would seek permission to take me to their flat in Geetanjali Apartments on Nepean Sea Road for hours of music and appetising khanaa. Suraiya was one of the most beautiful women I had ever seen. Daughter of a Nawabi family of Lucknow, as I remember, she had run away to marry the Ustad. She played tanpura for every concert in India and abroad as the two brothers, Ustad Moinuddin and his younger brother Ustad Aminuddin Dagar, sang rare compositions from the ancient music tradition of Dhrupad. When they started their school of Dhrupad in Bombay in 1964, they asked me to dance for their inauguration and I travelled from Bangalore with my musicians for the recital. After my performance, the renowned maestro Ustad Vilayat Khan took the stage with his sitar.

Ustad Vilayat Khan was quite a regular guest at my parental

Ustad Moinuddin Dagar & Ustad nasir Aminuddin Dagar
And Suraiya Dagar on Tanpura

home. I remember his small cute flat on Nepean Sea Road in Bombay, where he lived with his Bengali wife Monisha and young son, Shujaat. Their two daughters were not yet born. My association with Ustad Vilayat Khan carried well up to the time he shifted to Dehradun. Suffice it to say, growing up with such an eclectic mix of artistes was bound to leave a lasting impression on me for the rest of my life.

The power and resonance of dance and music are immeasurable. To reinforce life's purpose and motivation, to redefine what is good, auspicious and beautiful, and to return to ourselves in the knowledge of our own divinity, we need to shift our focus from crass materialism and vicious hyperbole to the calming influence of the performing arts.

The moment for a balanced relook has come. Today it may be more apt to say that if religions divides, the arts unite.

Chapter 6

Vishnu 'Why is Life Divine?'

It was 10 May 1983. Badrinath was covered in snow. From a heat-soaked Delhi, we took the road through Muzaffarnagar to Haridwar-Rishikesh and entered the Himalayan region. I never use the extra 's' as in Himalayas because the original word in Sanskrit already denotes plural, a conglomeration of snow-covered mountains. Back then, the roads were not double-lane, neither in such bad condition as now. With two night halts at Rishikesh and Srinagar in Uttarakhand, we arrived at the Garhwal Vikas Nigam in Badrinath. It was very rudimentary in those days, with almost no electricity or running water. My group of musicians and I had reached a good day-and-a-half early to acclimatise ourselves to the altitude.

Next morning, I walked 5 km to Mana. The distance is now 3 kms from Badrinath to Mana because the curving road has been straightened now. The last village on the Indian side just 40 km as the crow flies from the border with China. It was then a circuitous route, not straight like it is now. The IB check-post was small with friendly and hospitable people. We were offered tea and biscuits and as I sat on the low compound wall looking at the vast expanse of snow-covered empty space as far as the eye could see, I noticed a black dot on the snow. It was a person who was coming closer, every minute. It was a sadhu with bare minimum clothing, a black blanket draped on one shoulder, a chipiya or iron tong in one hand and with no footwear! His eyes were red as if drunk or angry, and as he came up within speaking distance, I offered a namaskaram and asked if he would like some tea. As he sipped his tea standing there by the wall, I asked where he was headed. 'Vasudhara,' he replied, curtly. It is a destination across vast expanses of snow, almost near the border where eight waterfalls create a magical view. The mythical city of Alkapuri where Kuber, the Divine treasurer has his headquarters, is said to be located atop the waterfalls.

I pointed to his bare feet asking if he needed footwear which the helpful IB men could provide. He did not answer but resumed his straight-backed walk across the snow-covered expanse. I turned for a moment to put away my teacup, and as I looked back, I did not see anything but the vast, empty snowy landscape. Where did he vanish? This was on 11 May. In the evening, we had wonderful darshan of Shri Badrinath after which I stood right there in front of the deity and danced the Dashaavatar, the chronological depiction of Vishnu's 10 incarnations.

The chief priest, Unniyal ji remembered me from my inaugural performance in 1983 at the Badrinath festival and all through my other three visits till 8 May 2013 when I danced in the Badrinath festival again!

On 12 May 1983, I was to dance on a makeshift stage in a pandal at 12 noon for about one-and-a-half hours. Following that was a Bhajan recital, and the entire programme had to be wound up before 4 pm to avoid cold winds or snowfall as in this part of the country, it becomes dark by 4.30 pm.

The Neelkanth and Nara-Narayan peaks on either side watched intensely as I danced connecting the divine in me to the

Divine. The central piece was my choreography of the sixteen names of Vishnu. Of course, Vishnu like every divinity in India has many titles, names and synonyms, each relating to a particular aspect, deed or incident. Vishnu is the one among the Trinity of Brahma, Vishnu and Mahesh (Shiva) entrusted with the task of nourishing and looking after the well-being of Creation, somewhat similar to the role of a mother. This particular group of sixteen names were all connected to our daily life.

I am constantly astonished by the range and richness of the imagination of those who joyfully dedicated every activity and action—however mundane—to Divine grace and enjoined succeeding generations to be grateful. As I danced this particular item, my musicians noticed that many amongst the audience, especially sadhus and women, were quickly jotting down the names with the action-activity for which it was suggested. It was set in raaga maalika, literally, a garland of sixteen raagas set to different rhythmic cycles. For those of you who enjoy the subtlety and variety of this novel, rather the ancient tradition of invoking the Divine, here are more details:

1. **Aushadhe Chintayet Visnum/ औषधे चिन्तयेद् विष्णुम्**

   When unwell or sick, when taking medicine becomes necessary, invoke the name VISHNU who is all-pervading, who removes the fetters of life.

2. **Bhojane ch Janaardanam/ भोजने च जनार्दनम्**

   Invoke Janaardana at the time when one sits down to a meal because Vishnu as all-pervasive Brahm creates and nourishes all Creation.

3. **Shayane Padmanaabham ch/ शयने पद्मनाभं च**

   For a restful night's sleep, invoke the name of Padmanaabha, He who has the Lotus of Creation sprouting from his navel as he reclines on the cosmic serpent Shesha.

4. **Vivaahe ch Prajaapatim/ विवाहे च प्रजापतिम्**
   Prajaapati is the divinity to be invoked at the time of marriage, because he blesses the couple with energy to produce progeny.
5. **Yuddhe Chakradharam Devam / युद्धे चक्रधरं देवं**
   In battle and war, one should direct the mind to Chakradhara, holding the weapon Discus—the chakra which cuts through everything in every direction as it rotates.
6. **Pravaase ch Trivikramam/ प्रवासे च त्रिविक्रमम्**
   While on a journey, the name of Trivikrama ensures safety and success. The episode refers to one in which Vishnu grew into the cosmic form covering the three worlds. It is full of wonderment and possibilities of human endeavour.
7. **Naaraayanam Tanutyaage/ नारायणं तनुत्यागे**
   As the last breath struggles to leave the body, as Death closes in every moment, let the mind focus on the name of Narayana, the Cosmic Being.
8. **Shridharam Priyasamgame/ श्रीधरं प्रियसंगमे**
   In the deep embrace of love, at the height of passion, in blissful moments with the beloved, let the mind recall the form of Shridhar, He who holds Shri, the most beautiful and charming Goddess Lakshmi in his embrace.
9. **Duhsvapne Smara Govindam/ दुःस्वप्ने स्मर गोविन्दं**
   When assailed by unpleasant dreams, direct your mind to focus on the name of Govinda—he who is the all-knowing source of Creation.
10. **Sankate Madhusudanam/ संकटे मधुसूदनम्**
    When demon Madhu attacked the recumbent Vishnu, he was killed at once, and from this incident, was the title Madhusoodana born, the destroyer of Madhu. Utter this name whenever in tricky, difficult or seemingly insurmountable situations.

11. **Kaanane Naarasimham ch/ कानने नारसिंहं च**
When traversing through deep, dense forests, recite the name of Narasimha, the fourth incarnation of Vishnu as the terrifying half-lion, half-man. He put an end to the arrogant King Hiranyakashipu in this form. The name alone ensures full safety from wild animals.

12. **Paavake Jalashaayinam/ पावके जलशायिन**
In case of a raging, engulfing fire, immediately think of Jalashaayina Vishnu lying on the bed of serpent Shesha in the deep ocean because water works as antidote to fire.

13. **Jalamadhye Varaaham ch/ जलमध्ये वराहं च**
If afraid of water or in a dire situation of being engulfed by water or drowning, invoke the name and image of Varaaha, wild boar, who rescued the drowning Earth from deep ocean. Varaaha is the third incarnation of Vishnu.

14. **Parvate Raghunandanam/ पर्वते रघुनन्दनम्**
Shri Ramachandra traversed many hills and mountains while searching for Sita, his wife. Therefore Raghunandana Ram, born in the family of his ancestor, King Raghu, would ensure unhindered journey over mountains.

15. **Pravaase Vaamanam Chaiva/ प्रवासे वामनं चैव**
While preparing for journey, pray to Vaamana, the fifth incarnation of Vishnu, who, after asking for space that would be enough to cover his three steps, grew into cosmic form covering Heaven with the first step, entire Earth with the second, and paused as his third step was suspended in space. He inquired where and how King Bali proposed to fulfil his promise to grant the three steps. That's when the arrogant King Bali bowed in humility. As Vaamana's third step was placed on Bali's head, he was pushed to Paatala, the netherworld. So, invoking the form and name of Vaamana ensures successful journey.

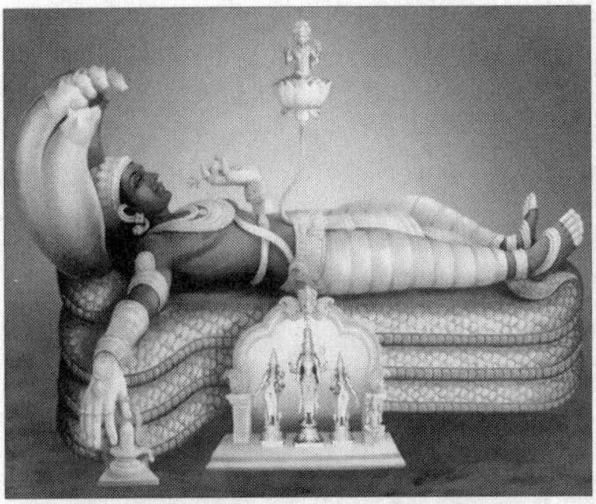

Shayane Padmanaabham ch/ शयने पद्मनाभं च

Pravaase ch Trivikramam/ प्रवासे च त्रिविक्रमम्

Duhsvapne Smara Govindam/ दुःस्वप्ने स्मर गोविन्दं

Sankate Madhusudanam/ संकटे मधुसूदनम्

Kaanane Naarasimham ch/ कानने नारसिंहं च

Paavake Jalashaayinam/ पावके जलशायिन

Jalamadhye Varaaham ch/ जलमध्ये वराहं च

Parvate Raghunandanam/ पर्वते रघुनन्दनम्

Pravaase Vaamanam Chaiva/ प्रवासे वामनं चैव

Sarvakaaryeshu Maadhavam/ सर्वकार्येषु माधवम्

16. Sarvakaaryeshu Maadhavam/ सर्वकार्येषु माधवम्

Maadhava has two beautiful meanings: Sweet as honey and husband of Maa Lakshmi. Concentrating on the name Maadhava throughout the day while attending to routine work and in every action proves beneficial.

This is a nice escape route for modern-day social networking computer and Google-dependent people who may not remember or carry the burden of 16 different names, meanings and occasions for invocation. Our ancestors were so much more open and considerate than we who cannot tolerate or understand each other's varied approach and thoughts.

Instead, they gave us the complete overview and made provisions for our over-burdened, agitating, forgetful minds. May these names grant good luck and peace to all.

Chapter 7

Sapta-nadi

The Seven Rivers of India

For conducting a religious ceremony, ritual or celebration, a certain litany of Sanskrit verses are recited which are common to almost all Hindus in India or in any part of the world. Water is one of the important elements in these rituals which is kept in a kumbh—pot made of either copper, peetal (an alloy) or even clay. The names of seven ancient rivers are chanted to invoke their presence in the pot.

गङ्गे च यमुने चैव गोदावरी सरस्वति।
नर्मदे सिन्धु कावेरी जलेऽस्मिन् संन्निधिं कुरु॥

In 2002 I was inspired to create Asmita, a new choreography in five parts, beginning with Bindu, the point of the beginning of cosmic creation. The second part was called Sapta-nadi, the seven rivers which is relevant here. I established their historical and spiritual identity by depicting one significant event and legend in dance with specially composed music. My dancers had to first get acquainted with the geography of that particular river, because to my great surprise and shock, none of them knew anything about

River-Dance

the rivers' udgam or birthplace and the significance and importance of their existence on the Indian subcontinent!

I often wonder if the modern education system still considers such information trivial. If Indians are eager to bathe in these rivers according to their socio-religious injunctions to wash away their accumulated sins, would it be too much to ask them to know more about these rivers and offer not only worship but also affection? We expect so much from them—pure water to quench our aeonic thirst, constant flow of water to wash away impurities, to irrigate land for vegetation, for agriculture and flora-fauna to survive, and generally to create a pleasant ambience for our enjoyment. We love our picnics and outings on a riverbank, because even a small stream of gurgling water gives us so much joy and peace. Our modern-day temperament is about wanting and expecting, not about giving and thanking!

So, I vigorously set about educating my group to recognise the need for such details. My own way of working on any idea or project is to create a big picture with as much information and detail as is possible to gather. I read, write, consult scholars, discuss and prepare a framework, then shortlist points to suit the tight narrative and duration of choreography. This method has given me a much wider scope to absorb and understand the concept in all its complexity and textures. Thus, my dancers got their lessons in the geo-historical context of seven rivers much to their amazement and delight.

While river Gangaa brought images of her descent from heaven to earth in response to Bhagirath's severe penance, river Yamunaa brought alive stories of Shri Krishna. The popular images in painting and sculptures, in music and dance, include the battle to remove river pollution as well as the Raas-lilaa with Raadha and the gopis on the night of the bright autumnal full moon on the Yamunaa river's verdant riverbank.

River Saraswati

The name pertains to the goddess of learning in arts and wisdom, as well as to the river mentioned in the Rig Veda. History tells us that great civilisations prospered on her banks, and some of the ruins that have been excavated in Lothal and

The Eternal Flow

Goddess Saraswati

Dholavira in Gujarat point to this. Some 1,500 years ago, the river is believed to have disappeared into the desert of what is today's Rajasthan and parts of Haryana. Satellite pictures have established her identity underground right up to Kutch at the tip of western Gujarat. Today, one can have her darshan only in one location above Mana village near the Himalayan region of Badrinath. In June 2013, I was dancing for the second time at the Badrinath festival just a week before a colossal tragedy struck. The festival had started with my programme in 1983, a fact reinforced by saffron-clad sadhus shouting 'Jai ho' at the end of my recital in 2013 and then pushing forward, telling everybody in the audience, 'Aap toh tees varshon pehle bhi aayee thi. Ab bhi aisi hee hain!' (You had also come 30 years ago; you are still the same.) The Rig Veda mentions the many Yajnas or sacred rituals performed on the banks of the Saraswati by Rishis whose ashrams dotted the banks. I recreated that scene complete with Vedic chanting as Saraswati the Goddess showered blessings.

रमणीयातिरमणीया ज्ञानदात्री सरस्वती।
मतिमती गुणमयी कलासौंदर्यशालिनी॥

More attractive than other goddesses, Saraswati is the giver of knowledge and intellect. She is Wisdom personified and has a brilliant aura of arts, aesthetics and beauty.

An ancient legend tells us of the beginning of time when Aadi-Shakti divided herself into five parts which became five goddesses: Raadha, Padma, Savitri, Durga and Saraswati. They manifested through the limbs of Shri Krishna, aka Shri Vishnu. Saraswati manifested from Shri Krishna's throat:

॥ कृष्णकण्ठोद्भवा सा च देवी सरस्वती॥
मंत्र- ॐ ऐं ह्रीं सरस्वत्यै नमः।

This chant was given to Sage Valmiki by Shri Vishnu. By reciting this chant, Sage Valmiki attained the power of poetic creation by which he wrote the great epic, Ramayana. Other rishis like Veda Vyas, Vasishtha, Vishwamitra and Shaunak achieved great results and were able to contribute significantly to India's ancient spiritual and literary traditions.

In a shloka in the Brihaddharma Purana:

Goddess Saraswati instructs Veda Vyaasa, 'I am (the) personified power of expression in the Ramayana composed by Sage Valmiki; by my grace, go and read it.'

Another instance of the power of worshipping Saraswati is of poet Kalidaas (4th century AD) who transformed from an ignorant illiterate into an enlightened poet.

The only example of Saraswati both as a goddess and a river is found in the Rig Veda. As a goddess, she grants pure mind and inspires the speaking of truth.

The name Saraswati includes the word Sar (in Sanskrit), meaning water—therefore, a river which is full of water.

As usual, in Sanskrit literature, Saraswati as goddess and river has many synonyms viz Jayashree, Vak, Shaaradaa, Bhaarati, Vaani among several other.

The Rig Veda also mentions two special names, Vaaginivati and Ritavari.

From ancient times, the riverbanks were the best spots to establish ashrams and hermitages where daily rituals of offering homage to the goddess were practised through yajnas and homams. It is believed that banks of the river Saraswati were crowded with ashrams of great rishis and gurus.

The sixty-first sukta of the sixth mandal of the Rig Veda has fourteen richas which is called Saaraswat-Sukta. Every sukta has a presiding deity and a rishi who are to be invoked before chanting. In the Saaraswat-Sukta, the presiding deity is Goddess Saraswati and the rishi is Bharadwaj. Here Saraswati is invoked in both forms—as goddess and as river. As goddess, she is shown in a golden chariot who destroys enemies. As river, she nourishes.

Another mantra (chant) praises the river as always being full of water, sweet and strength giving. This river doesn't brook any obstacles as she rushes forward creating a huge sound.

As Vak Devi (Goddess of sound and language), she has seven meters like the Gayatri and as a river, she is one of the seven sisters including Gangaa.

At the end of the Saraswat-Sukta, the rishi invokes and prays to Saraswati, 'Oh Goddess who fills the earth and heaven with effulgence, protect us from anti-Gods, and from those who demean our rituals. Do not leave us in a pitiable state but bless us with wealth to fulfil our duties and thus gain merit.'

I often wonder and try to understand the popular belief about Pandits and scholars that they must remain needy and poor. Surprisingly, these chants make it clear how, in ancient times too, the situation was the same, albeit with two differences. First, wealth was needed to perform rituals and yajnas which were for the common good, unlike today when everything is for personal gain. Second, the kingdoms and rulers of those small or large states situated on the banks of river Saraswati provided enough wealth, gifts, etc. with which the ceremonies could be performed regularly and without hindrance.

Among the ancient civilisations of the world, India's Saraswati Civilisation is perhaps the oldest. Archaeological finds of cities like Lothal, Dholavira in Gujarat have brought up astounding artefacts and revealed perfect city planning. It can be argued that because most ashrams were on the banks of the Saraswati where the Vedic traditions, teachings and rituals were carried out, the river acquired the form of the Goddess of learning, knowledge and arts.

The idol of Saraswati has four arms which depict super-human beings and divinities. In her three arms, she holds the four Vedas, rosary (aksha maala) and small water pot (kamandal), while the fourth is held in benediction (abhaya). She is clad in bright white garments denoting purity and is seated on a white lotus. Every divine being in Indian thought is depicted with a mount. Saraswati has the white swan, again a symbol of purity, pavitrata and sense of discretion, Vivek.

It is believed that the Saraswati idol was first conceived at the time of the Kushan and Shung dynasties. The oldest idol of

Saraswati as a goddess is found in 2 BCE, about 2,400 years ago in the time of the Kushans. By the 9th century AD, she was also established as the Goddess of music and the arts, the symbol of which is the Veena which she holds as if playing music.

Sometimes, the peacock is shown as her mount, perhaps because in Indian music texts, the sound of each of the seven notes is compared to the call of a bird or animal. The first note, shadja (Sa) resembles the sound made by the peacock, Mayur.

Saraswati is also worshipped in Japan and South-East Asian countries as Goddess of knowledge and arts. She occupies special place of honour in Jain religion where she is known as Shrutdevata, and in Buddhism as Pragnya Paramita.

River Sindhu

Like her other sisters, the river Sindhu is born from the higher altitudes of Himalayan range. She is truly like the ocean at places which are now in Pakistan and where Alexander, better known as Sikander is supposed to have given up his idea of going forward to conquer lands on the other side of this vast water body. Popular belief has an interesting explanation for the word 'Hindu' as being the mispronunciation of the word Sindhu. So all those who lived on the opposite bank and beyond were Sindhu=Hindu! Similarly, the State of Assam in North-East India is derived from 'Ahom', the royal dynasty from Burma which ruled the land. This is an example of how pronunciations change over time. Today, the Sindhu can be seen only below the capital city of Ladakh from where it flows into the mountainous regions of Pakistan. For one of my dance productions, I recreated the scene of Porus and Alexander. King Porus surrendered after his defeat but demanded that he be treated not as prisoner of war but as a king. Sikander heeded this dignified request and not only released but befriended the self-respecting king. My dancers were surprised to learn the power of self-respect, Aatma-Samman and courage of conviction.

History teaches us many good lessons but alas, we scarcely preserve these in our collective or individual memory.

River Kaaveri

In the line-up of sacred rivers of India, the northern rivers seem to score over others, but the Kaaveri River, which flows south of the Vindhyas, firmly and effortlessly stands her ground in the realm of sacredness because many of India's most sacred and spiritual centres and grand temples dot the banks of the Kaaveri. Emerging from Tala-Kaaveri, the great centre of pilgrimage in Karnataka state, she flows through Karnataka and Tamil Nadu before joining the mercurial waters of the Bay of Bengal. But it is at Srirangam that she acquires the utmost character and sanctity where she splits into two streams forming one of the most beautiful river islands of Srirangam where the magnificent temple of Sri Ranganatha Swamy stands. The island is sacred to both Vaishnavites and Shaivites. Sri Ranganatha is one of the forms of Shri Vishnu and thus the temple of Sri Ranganatha Swamy is the centre of worship for all sects of Vaishnavism. Some distance away stands one of the five sacred places for Shaivites in the realm of God Shiva's anthropomorphic form, he is worshipped as representing the first element—water. The water element is represented here as Jambukeshwar Mahadev where a perennial stream anoints the Shivalinga.

The legend of Andal, the young and beautiful daughter of Periyalwar, first among the 64 Alwars (Vaishnavite saints of southern India) still occupies the imagination of the Vaishnavs of south India. She was deeply in love with Sri Ranganatha and imagined herself to be His bride. Songs sung by her describing her dream of her marriage to the Lord of her heart form an important part of the repertory in Bharatanatyam. It was her duty to prepare the garland offered to Him every day. Immersed as she was in her ecstasy, she wore the garland as if the Lord had placed it round her neck. She sang and danced until it was time for her father to take it to the temple along with all the other puja paraphernalia. As the garland was placed on the Lord, a long, black hair became visible. There was chaos and shouts of blasphemy. Andal was summoned and when she was questioned, she accepted the fact and before the eyes of the enraged crowd of priests and devotees, she merged with the Lord's idol. This deeply moving legend compares with the north Indian legend of the saint-poetess Meera of Rajasthan who merged with the idol of Shri Dwarkadheesh, another form of the God Vishnu or Krishna in Gujarat.

Chapter 8

Water Water Everywhere

I am fascinated by water, the primal element in creation. It is at once inviting and challenging. It can feel like velvet or a knife, translucent like the Moon, shining like a mirror, or suddenly dark and foreboding, heavy with the secret of Creation. It is one of the 12 symbols and names in our horoscopes. Ever since my father carried me on his back as he swam in the 'Fairy Pool' in Panchmadhi in Madhya Pradesh when I was just 4 years old, I loved the feel of cool water and refused to get off his back even at the end of a full hour. Then I graduated to an inflated rubber tyre on which I would sit like a water nymph, steering my water chariot by enthusiastically flailing my arms in the water. By the age of 12, I had learnt swimming in Bombay where I was born and educated. Ever since, I have swum in flowing rivers, lakes, under waterfalls and oceans. I am narrating some of my most memorable trysts with water here.

My oceanic experiences include swimming in the Atlantic Ocean in 14° Celsius temperature at the resort town of Ogunquit in Maine on USA's West Coast. The icy cold North Sea on the northern shore of Belgium was another chilling experience, but I will never forget the most wonderful experience of swimming like a fish in the velvety waters of the Adriatic Sea at Dubrovnik in erstwhile Yugoslavia. In India, swimming in the waters at the tri-junction at Kanyakumari at the southernmost tip of India where the Indian Ocean accepts tributes from the Bay of Bengal and the Western Sea has always been magical. The spot where the river Chandrabhaga meets the ocean near Konark in Odisha is deeply entrenched in history and mythology. The beach falls sharply at Jagannathpuri on the country's eastern coast. The beaches of Goa and of Kovalam in Kerala are the dream of every tourist, but I have enjoyed the sea in these two places when they were quiet and welcoming. Of the many lakes, the most noteworthy and frightening was Lake Michigan at Chicago! I enjoyed a swim in perfectly salubrious waters while on a picnic with the Indian Consul General and his family. A fortnight later, when I went back for yet another recital at the National Public Library, I insisted on a similar outing the next morning. It was early afternoon and the sun was shining. As they laid out the picnic hamper and sat back chatting, I ran into the water and swam out humming a smart tune, feeling like a mermaid. Within moments, I felt under-currents pulling me further out. The water underneath was icy cold and the currents were strongly gripping my limbs. I tried to look back and shout, but nothing happened. Providentially, I was swept close to those thick wooden logs which indicated the limit after which Lake Michigan was free to swallow you. I held on to one with all the strength I could muster, embracing one with both arms as I would, a lover. After a few seconds of reprieve and deep breathing and with determination not to drown, I swam back with strong strokes to the security of terra firma. My friends had no inkling of my plight. They were happy to recount my swimming prowess to others because I

Sonal diving in the water (left); Seated on a rock

didn't open my mouth about the incident till much later. After all, one should not puncture certain illusions, especially when the reference point is you.

I have also swum in some of the Indian rivers—in the Narmadaa at Maheshwar and also at Omkareshwar, in the Kaveri river at Srirangapatnam in Tamil Nadu, and in the Krishna near Jamkhandi, in the Tungabhadra region near Hampi in Karnataka. I have also swum in the Yamunaa at Vrindavan in Uttar Pradesh, at the Pindari Gangaa at Karna-Prayag in Uttarakhand and of course, in the Sangam at Prayagraj in Uttar Pradesh; but the list is incomplete without mentioning the innumerable streams and waterfalls across India. While enjoying whitewater rafting on the Gangaa, I had a sudden impulse to jump off the raft in the swiftly flowing river, a long way above Rishikesh. To the dismay of my co-rafters, I disappeared from sight. I had let myself be taken in by the Gangaa, becoming one with the flow while chanting shlokas to propitiate her. I floated right up to Lakshman-Jhoola to the amazed and amused shouts of scores of onlookers standing on the bridge. I headed towards the sandy bank and was relieved to find myself on dry land again.

Chapter 9

Gangaa the Loka-maata

Gangaa literally means that which flows, goes, continues… In that sense, every river is Gangaa. The origins of rivers are also treated as sacred points where people offer worship and gratitude. I have many compositions on rivers of India in my dance repertory which include narratives and historical proof.

The legend of Gangaa's descent from Swarg or heaven is cherished by generations. The river had been brought down from heaven specifically to revive the world order and to release the

Gangaavtaran

Counting Rosary on banks of Gangaa in Varanasi

curse on a group of a hundred arrogant princes who had been burnt to ashes by a great rishi for having mocked and insulted a saint who was sitting deep in meditation. Bhagirath, the successor to the throne, had to perform long penance to please the celestial river and request her to descend to earth to liberate the souls of his ancestors, the princes so that life could flourish again. Gangaa accepted the request but cautioned the king to prepare an adequately strong base to contain her torrential waters which would otherwise demolish everything on earth and flow into the netherworld. Hence Bhagirath engaged in penance to please Shiva who accepted the challenge. As the waters whooshed down on earth, Shiva opened up his long, matted hair and stood firm to receive the descent of Gangaa's waters. As she fell on his head, he quickly tied his locks, thus containing the waters and allowing them to flow gradually and gracefully. The symbolism of the legend is so obvious yet, we have become totally oblivious to the import of the message. Shiva's long, matted hair represent dense forests of the Himalaya or any mountain, hill, plateau from which water flows down. If the forests are decimated as has been done for some time now, water will simply gush out without any check or balance, and play havoc with everything in its way. The firmly planted feet of Shiva point towards firmness of resolve to save the earth from disastrous floods and all the concomitant problems such events will bring in their wake.

Let us turn our attention to the honour accorded to the rivers by calling them Loka-Maata. Maata is 'Mother' and Loka means 'world' or 'people'. River is Mother to all. Her waters nourish agriculture and forests and satiate collective thirst. The flow of cool water indicates flow of life from birth to death. Just as a river journeys from her birthplace to the point of submergence in the ocean and then to new forms as vapour to fill rain-bearing clouds with water which release rain to once again fill water bodies to allow undiminished flow of rivers to nourish the earth and people, our life too merges with the all-pervasive energy and gets transformed into new forms and shapes to keep the world order going. Great civilisations grew and prospered on the banks of rivers like the Nile, Euphrates and Tigris, and Gangaa-Yamunaa-Sindhu-Kaveri-Godaavari-Narmadaa in India. How can we ever

Iconography of River Gangaa seated on Makara

Descent of river Gangaa on Bhagavan Shiva's open locks

forget Saraswati which disappeared underground after nourishing civilisations like Harappa, Mohenjo-daro, Dholavira, and Lothal?

If we refuse to hear the voice of our Mother, Loka-Maata, in the vivifying cool waters of the river, we will suffer further miseries and misfortunes as we are witnessing in present times. Over the last few decades, we have insensitively ravaged and been disrespectful to our rivers. We have taken them for granted and exploited them shamelessly. Yet, the Loka-Maata has forgiven us time and again. However, she may not always pardon us.

Chapter 10

Yamunaa Witness to Krishna-leela

Yamunaa emerges from the high altitude glacier of Yamunotri and flows down through the plains of northern India till it meets and merges with the Gangaa at Prayagraj. Her waters are dark blue unlike the opaque, translucent whitish waters of the Gangaa. The Yamunaa is steeped in romantic imagery, more so than any other Indian river, simply because she flows through Krishna-land, the Vraja-bhoomi or abode of Shri Krishna and Raadha. She is the prime witness to numerous 'Leelas' of Krishna, his mischief, love, and playful acts of subjugating dark demonic forces. It is indeed deeply confusing to separate stories from history, legend from reality, but then, don't we all experience such situations in life where separation of the unreal from the real becomes redundant? Therefore, although Krishna of the *Srimadbhagvat*: his biography, the epic *Mahabharata* and the *Bhagavad Gita* refer to the same persona, and we are left in a perpetual state of disbelief, rather suspension of belief wondering 'how a baby can suck out the life-breath from the ogress Putana's poisoned breast, or how could he perform miraculous feats of wrestling with Kaaliya the Cobra-King in the deep waters of the

On banks of Yamunaa, lonely Raadha playing on Krishna's flute, after he has left Vrindavan, never to return

Yamunaa and emerge dancing on the enormous hood and then tease the nubile young gopis (milkmaids) of Vrindavan by stealing their clothes while they bathed in the refreshing, cool clear waters of the Yamunaa?'

The Yamunaa forms an integral thread of all the Krishna narratives from babyhood to boyhood and all through adolescence. Rows of Kadamba trees on the banks of Yamunaa, the call of his flute, and the myriad moods of loveplay between Raadha and Krishna, Krishna and the gopis, besides the heart-wrenching love of his foster mother, Yashoda and the unwavering faith of his buddies, the Gopa-sakha (cowherd boys) are all watched silently by the river Yamunaa, with her dark waters guarding many secrets. The poets have not stopped singing and writing about how and why and when the waters turned dark. Was it because of Kaaliya's poison or was it to hide the naked bathing gopis from the searing, unrelenting gaze of Krishna, or when the gopis shed copious tears as Krishna bade farewell, their tears awash with the dark kaajal (collyrium) from their dark eyes and their dark, heavy sighs of sorrow?

Yamunaa's family tree is impressive. She is called Soorya-putri or Ravi-suta, daughter of the Sun God, hence sister of Yama, the guardian Dikpala of the southern direction, also the God of Death, and Transformation. Death here signifies the cessation of old and useless baggage of action-reaction-biases-prejudices and other such similar emotions collected during a lifetime.

Yama also means discipline, adherence to self control and the system of maintaining balance. In Yogic parlance, the first step of Ashtaanga Yoga (eight limbs of Yoga) is Yama i.e. discipline. In the iconography of the river Yamunaa, her mount the tortoise is ever present. It is, therefore, not surprising that they abound in that stretch of the river which flows by Shri Krishna's birthplace Mathura.

Yamunaa and her narratives are an integral part of the repertory of any Indian dance form, especially Bharatanatyam, Odissi, Kathak and Kuchipudi, where a solo dancer tackles one or more such popular episodes, many of them drawn from the life of Krishna. Yamunaa has been witness to some of the most significant and philosophical discourses and incidents which have illuminated our minds beyond imagination. One such episode tells us about the secret desire of every woman of Vrindavan to have Krishna as her husband. They are all madly in love with Krishna and they playfully tease each other while bathing in the cool blue waters, unmindful of the goings on around their clothes and ornaments which lie on the bank. When the time comes to return home, they walk out of the river still intoxicated with passion and desire. Their search for their clothes proves futile. Incredulous, they run hither and thither, now suddenly embarrassed and feeling totally exposed.

The dancer creates the Yamunaa with ripples and waves, and also with fish and tortoise which abound in the river. With flowing steps, and rippling arm and hand movements, the dancer establishes Yamunaa's presence on stage. Dexterity in technique alone does not and cannot do justice to the creation of imagery and scenes that are replete with elements of nature, characters and changing situations. These are ideally presented through body postures or anga-bhangi and through hand gestures or hasta-mudra and facial expressions or bhaava. This is akin to saying that just by knowing the alphabet and grammar, one cannot become a poet! The dancer has to dive into the flow of the story, letting go of her individual persona and ego. The game of light and shade in expression has to be played with a clear understanding of the nuances and small details demanded by the story. Exaggeration has to be avoided. Even a word from the poem or song has to be addressed at the level of weight and meaning of the word to convey its contextual meaning and deeper import.

India and Indians have never differentiated or labeled its various beliefs. Every belief is supported by faith and everyone's faith and belief are as good as anyone else's. Folk, classical and tribal legends merge at a point of majesty and spatial vision of the

Pensive Krishna on banks of Yamunaa

cosmic scheme. Also of interest particularly to those familiar with iconography, is the parallel between Shiva's androgynous form of Ardhanareeshwara and Vishnu-Krishna's Krishna-Kaali form. Convergence is the key to understanding some preliminary principles of the Indic mind.

Let me conclude with a beautiful legend which has a concrete presence even today. One hot afternoon, as Krishna lay in Raadha's lap under a flower-laden Kadamba tree that was swaying gently in the cool breeze from Yamunaa's incessantly singing waters, Raadha saw two figures from afar. On closer scrutiny, she could recognise them as her mother-in-law Jatila meaning knotted or complex and her sister-in-law Kutila, another word for someone who is devious and wicked. Krishna made no move

Iconography representation of river Yamunaa going to meet krishna–visual interpretation from a Vaishnava Pushti-Marg painting

to get up. Raadha too was calm. The women approached, cursing and abusing Raadha for having shamed the family, the entire clan and village by openly and brazenly carrying on with the rascal, Krishna. They had seen Raadha with a supine figure in her lap bearing a peacock feather and wearing a yellow dhoti. Today, they thought, they were going to shame her and expose her misdeeds. Spluttering and muttering loudly, they arrived and to their surprise saw the idol of their Kula-Devi (chief deity) KAALI. Stupefied, they could only fall at Raadha's feet. Since then, among the plethora of temples in Vrindavan, it is this small but powerful temple of Krishna-Kaali where the black stone idol of Krishna is worshipped as Kaali, complete with long sari, tilak and ornaments.

Chapter 11

Story of Narmadaa

Narmadaa divides North and South India geographically, but also connects the two by the sheer magnitude and magic of her personality and nobility. Legend attributes Narmadaa with great powers of purification, so much so that once a year, river Gangaa, heavy and burdened with the sins of people bathing in her waters, comes to Narmadaa to bathe and wash away her own burdens, to go back lighter, and once again be ready to absorb people's dark thoughts and deeds. Narmadaa is supposed to have emerged from the sacred navel of the Great God Shiva. Any wonder then if she is honoured with an entire Puraan dedicated to her: the Narmadaa Puraan.

The Gondwana Plateau lies between the ancient mountain ranges of Satpuda and Vindhyachal, one of the oldest landmasses unlike the Atlantis which is supposed to have sunk into the ocean. From the Gondwana Plateau, emerge Narmadaa and Tapti which flow westward, Sone that flows northwards and Maha, which flows eastwards. Narmadaa originates at Amarkantak where a thin trickle of the river is like a little girl just finding her balance. I remember easily hopping across this tiny rivulet when

I was only six years old! Very quickly, she acquires strength and cuts across Marble Rocks near Jabalpur at Bhedaghat. One of the few temples dedicated to 64 Yoginis is located there, now in ruins yet still filled with powerful vibrations. The Narmadaa here forms a deep gorge and her torrential flow carves those hard rocks into Shivalingas in every size imaginable. They are appropriately called Narmadeshwar Mahadeva, Lord of Narmadaa. Flowing majestically, she is the only river with the unique honour of hosting two of the 12 Jyotirlingas, the effulgent pre-historic forms of Shiva at Omkareshwar and Amaleshwar on the opposite bank. Maheshwar is another place of historic importance among numerous others and was known to be Devi Ahilyabai Holkar's favourite city. Devi Ahilyabai Holkar's Tri-Centennary celebrations are afoot. She was an enlightened and extraordinary ruler of Malwa who received unstinted honour and respect from other rulers of the day. She shifted Malwa's capital from Indore to Maheshwar. It is now a throbbing hub of fine cotton and silk textiles.

Birth of Narmadaa at Amarkantak, Madhya Pradesh

Omakareshwar Jyotirling Temple on Banks of River Narmadaa

Synonyms for the Narmadaa are found in Amarkosh, a Sanskrit thesaurus wherein the entries on 1.0.132 list Reva, Somodbhava and Mekalkanya. According to one legend from the Skandpuraan, God Shiva asks the river to flow southwards, for which reason, Narmadaa is also known as Gangaa of the south. In the chapter 'Revakhand of Skandpuraan' there is a reference to the three rivers: Gangaa, Reva (Narmadaa) and Saraswati, which are supposed to have emanated from the Rudra form of God Shiva. Special connection to the trinity of Gods Brahma, Vishnu and Mahesh is established by connecting the three river goddesses to them. They are known as manifestations of the feminine forms of the three gods. Thus, the Gangaa is known as Vaishnavi-Moorti, the Narmadaa as Saivi-Moorti and the Saraswati as Brahmi-Moorti.

In the Mahabharata, we find reference to the Narmadaa 18 times, out of which I refer to the two below:

When the ritual of Rajasooya yajna was to be performed to establish sovereignty over various kingdoms of India, Sahadev, the fourth younger brother of the Pandava king Yudhishthira, went in southern direction. He travelled towards the river Narmadaa after victory over the Sek and Aparsek kingdoms.

The second reference is made by Sage Dhaumya, the royal and hereditary priest and Guru of the royal Pandava family. He refers to the river Narmadaa flowing from east to west through the kingdom of Aanurta, which is now the northern part of Gujarat. There are several such references to this great river which are like the references to the river Gangaa both in popularity and sacredness.

Legends describe the descent of Narmadaa from heaven somewhat like the legend of the river Gangaa. It is believed that back in ancient times, there was no river on the entire Indian subcontinent. Shiva, pleased by the intense penance offered by Hiranyateja for 14,000 years, asked the river Narmadaa to descend for the common good of the people.

I also found another deeply interesting episode of great significance which concerns a famous debate between the brilliant scholar, Mandana Mishr and Shankaracharya who came from Kaaladi in the state of Kerala in south India. He charted the path of establishing Sanatana Dharma or the Eternal Way, by challenging scholars and seers of different philosophies and views. This famous debate took place on the banks of Narmadaa over several weeks before Mandana Mishr finally accepted defeat. But not yet, said his equally learned wife Ubhaya Bharati, who was placed as the referee, umpire or moderator-anchor if her role can be described in today's parlance. As his wife, she had the right to pose a question for Shankaracharya. If he failed, defeat would be his. Bharati asked the ascetic Shankara about the experience of sexual love. Asking for a grace period of one year to be able to answer, Shankara left.

When he and his disciples saw lamentations for a recently

dead king, Shankara knew what he had to do. By the Siddhi, mystical powers of Parakaaya-pravesh, he abandoned his physical body in a nearby cave, instructing the disciples to guard it well, and entered the inert body of the king which came alive to the utter astonishment and delight of the queens and the royal household. Great celebrations were ordered while Shankara took zealously to learning the secrets of sexual love with the queens. As the year drew to a close, Shankara re-entered his own body in the cave and marched off to answer Bharati. He was able to describe the experience in detail so that Bharati joined her husband in acknowledging defeat and accepted the supremacy of Shankara's path of Sanatana Dharma, the principle of Advaita.

It was not easy to mould this episode into dance because I had to observe both caution and balance in depicting the pleasures of the flesh. Passion and desire and the many shades of sexual love need a deep understanding and a delicate touch which are the fruits of a lifelong Sadhana! Dancers should ideally evoke the Rasa-bhaava by not going overboard but describe it by economy of intense internalized emotions. Less is always more!

The Danger

Although we educated Indians, have perhaps become more aware of the environment as a living and precious entity and hold countless discourses and debates on a variety of topics such as the paucity of potable water, we mindlessly continue polluting our rivers and lakes. While pilgrimages to various places of worship on river banks are considered sacred, throwing non-biodegradable rubbish like polythene, plastic and styrofoam into rivers has also become normal activity. The sound of rippling water is muffled on mountain slopes and valleys, whether in rural or urban areas and our aqua life is dying. Algae and water hyacinths have covered more than half of our water bodies, not sparing even the still-water pools on river banks. Unless people i.e. society seriously works, puts in collective effort to conserve and cleanse water bodies, rivers, lakes, we may face serious crisis in near future by which time the problem may become unsolvable.

त्वदीय पादपंकजम्
नमामि देवि नर्मदे

We bow at your lotus feet
O Goddess Narmadaa

Chapter 12

Godaavari

Among the seven rivers of India whose names and presence are invoked at the beginning of every auspicious sacred ceremony, Godaavari has the distinction of hosting the Kumbh Mela on her banks at Nasik, Maharashtra. The Kumbh, held at Prayaagraj, the old name for the current Allahabad, is on the banks of the confluence of Gangaa, Yamunaa and the invisible but ever-present Saraswati, while the Godaavari is one of the three hostesses of that incredible festival held every four years in rotation in Haridwar on the banks of Gangaa, on the banks of Kshipra in Ujjain (MP) and in Nasik on banks of Godaavari.

Millions of people throng the Kumbh Mela, not necessarily out of faith or devotion but also to enjoy the exhilarating atmosphere of collective energy filling every bit of the environment. These places become like cities of tents where lakhs of pilgrims, sadhus and visitors are accommodated. Day and night merge with equal resonance of chanting, merry-making, announcements for lost-and-found, kirtans, loud discussions, satsangs and religious discourses.

I was curious to understand the undeniable sanctity attached

As described in the Ramayana, abduction of Sita by Raavan happened in Panchavati on the banks of River Godaavari

to the Kumbh which, when understood, opens up vistas of the richness of life on earth as is in the cosmos. What is good and life-nurturing on earth is equally good and life-giving in the solar systems. So, here is the myth, story or legend of the Kumbh, whatever you may choose to call it.

'Kumbh' means pitcher. It has several layers of connotations that make it an integral and significant part of our ceremonies. Kumbh or its other synonyms like ghada in Hindi, not only refer to the actual pot made of metal or earth but point to the human body and to the universe as well. An ancient Sanskrit verse defines Poorna and Shoonya—fullness and emptiness—through the analogy of the pitcher which when held up against the sky can signify emptiness or void, but when dipped in the ocean would signify poorna, fullness. At the time of cremation an earthen pitcher is carried on the left shoulder of the person who has to light the pyre. The pitcher is perforated by a single hole from which water i.e. Jeevan also meaning 'Life' seeps out. After completing the circumambulation, the pitcher is thrown on the ground to break it, signifying the breaking of earthly bonds of which the body is the main instrument.

In our story of the Kumbh, we have to turn our eyes to the scene where gods and anti-gods are busy at work. They are churning the Ksheera-sagar or the Milky Ocean, symbolising Creation. Both groups are in search of Amrit, the elixir of immortality. They have requested Shri Vishnu to extend support for stabilising the churning rod. The God appears in the form of the cosmic tortoise or koorma and offers support. This is the second incarnation among 10 known as Dashaavtar. The churning rod, Mount Mandaar is placed on the enormous and firm back of the cosmic tortoise. The great snake Vaasuki is persuaded to be the churning rope. The anti-Gods have chosen to hold the cobra head while the Gods are clearly better off with the tail. As they churn, poisonous fumes from Vaasuki's foaming hoods distress the impatient anti-Gods. However, as they continue to work diligently and one by one, thirteen divine gifts emerge from the depths of ocean. These are: conch; moon; kaustubh jewel; airawat elephant; uchhichravas horse; Goddess Shri; wish-fulfilling tree Parijat; celestial healer Dhanvantari; garland of victory, vyjayanti; celestial dancers Rambha, Menaka and Tilottama; divine bow sharnga; and celestial wine Varuni. The first to emerge is the deadly poison Halahala, the collective negativity and cosmic toxin which God Shiva Mahadeva drank, containing it in his throat. Now the churning really gathers speed as the fourteenth and final outcome of this arduous exercise was awaited. Slowly the pitcher of Amrit emerges. In the ensuing mayhem, the anti-gods got the better of the gods snatching the pitcher away. They had to be stopped before consuming it and becoming immortal which would throw the cosmic balance out of control. As a group of anti-gods was trying to get away, their haste was arrested by a vision of peerless beauty and seductive grace. They stood rooted as the enchanting vision came closer and engaged them in conversation, asking them in a silver bell-like tinkling voice why they were in such hurry! God Shri Vishnu as Mohini held their attention. Winning their trust, she offered to mediate and give equal share to both groups. Mohini succeeded in serving all the Amrit to the Gods. Four drops of Amrit had fallen on earth as the battle to take possession of the Kumbh was raging. Legend points to those four sacred spots on earth where the Kumbh Mela is now held. Devotees bathe in the sacred waters of these rivers in the firm belief of imbibing an atom of that Amrit! We too have the Amrit within us, yet we need concrete proof to believe that we are made of unbreakable stuff called faith and that we possess the elixir and divinity within ourselves.

At the time of staging the dance-drama Amrit-Manthan, choreographed by me and performed by my students in 1985, strange things happened. One of the Asuras or anti-Gods became

Shree Vishnu as Mohini the Enchantress holding the Kumbh(pot) of Elixir of Immortality

Modern-day Mohini holding pot of Amrita

over-enthusiastic when he saw his current ladylove as Apsara Rambha. He left the imaginary rope, caught her hand and began dancing with her. Another one of the dancers playing God had the presence of mind to intervene and push him back to the ranks of the anti-gods, much to the delight of the audience which saw the steps as well-choreographed comic relief. I can't even count the number of such confused snafus in that production, but we carried on, as did the musicians and my role as Mohini brought the house down. Much can be said about quick thinking on stage without which dance can turn into a totally unintended comedy.

In Sage Valmiki's Ramayana, as in many Indian epics and Puranas, we see India's sacred geography coming alive. Invariably, the main characters of the story travel through the length and breadth of the country taking us, the readers, along with them through forests and valleys, over mountains and across rivers. Not physically, yet, through the mind's eye, I have thus seen many beautiful places with the satisfaction of actually having been there and known them intimately. So, when I read the description of Panchavati in the Ramayana, I was eager to visit the place where Shri Rama and Devi Sita spent some of the happiest days together even though in exile and bereft of royal comforts. 'Panchavati' means a verdant grove created by five giant Banyan trees. The area is on the banks of river Godaavari, which emerges from a spot near Trimbakeshwar near the city of present-day Nashik in Maharashtra. This is where Shri Rama and Devi Sita spent the happiest days of their conjugal life protected by younger brother Lakshmana. This is also where the demoness, Shurpanakha tried to lure Shri Rama and Lakshmana but was humiliated. Her bitter complaint and sorry state enraged her brother, Ravana, king of Lanka. He sent uncle Maricha as a golden deer to entice Devi Sita and to remove Shri Rama and Lakshmana from her presence. He succeeded in carrying Devi Sita away to Lanka. My group depicted this with aplomb and conviction. I made even Shurpanakha look believable as a woman attracted to a handsome young man which was natural. Rather than pure black and white, I am interested in the grey areas where human psychology and relationships play out.

The temple of Trimbakeshwar where the Godaavari originates is also one of the twelve Jyotirlingams, the most sacred place for worshippers of Shiva Mahadeva. Interestingly, the Godaavari is also called Gautami because of the legend in which Sage Gautama, by worshipping God Shiva Mahadeva, received the boon by which the Gangaa's waters would flow underground emerging near Gautama's Ashram. The Rishi could then purify the Ashram with the water to absolve the sin of killing a crow, albeit unwittingly. Today, I have seen many among the educated, literate, liberated rich or middle-class, expressing disdain for the welfare of birds and animals, trees and flowers. Such legends should serve as examples of jeeva-daya: compassion for all sentient beings which includes every living thing on our planet.

The Godaavari or Gautami is the second longest river after the Gangaa on the Indian subcontinent. She is also known as Southern Ganges, or Dakshina Gangaa. Originating only 80 km from the Arabian Sea, she almost whimsically changes her mind and flows eastward through Maharashtra, Telangana and Andhra Pradesh to meet the Bay of Bengal! Reading the characteristics of each river, should it surprise us if a river is compared to a woman? Both, indeed are moody, temperamental, and given to whims and fancies but are always life-giving, life-nourishing and indispensable!

Chapter 13

Why I am 'Dwijaa', Twice Born

In the 2013 production of my Indic-Greek dance-drama 'When the Gods Meet' in Bangalore, I grilled my dancers during rehearsals. To be able to do cartwheels, somersaults and many other demanding movements because physical fitness is essential. Unlike what we see in dance reality shows on television where dancers jump, fall, skip, skate, leap, gyrate, pass through fiery hoops, twirl in space when hinged to wires like trapeze artistes in a circus, classical dancers have to be able to do all these and much more on stage without any help. For example, cartwheel movements on toes while fully seated, half-seated, bending forwards and backwards and to the sides or circular, also combined with classical dance steps in sync with the rhythms of complicated taal-cycle, and hand gestures, eye movements expressing different moods have to flow effortlessly during stage presentations. There cannot be even a moment's respite on stage. Props have to be worked with that in mind, placed in spots pre-determined to catch light or be in the dark corner as required because a carelessly placed stage prop can spell disaster for not only the production, but also for a dancer who might trip, fall and get injured.

Physical fitness flows from a strong and determined mind. Although Indian classical dancers nowadays have become more aware of the body, there is an invisible cut-off line beyond which they do not seem to progress. If they do, their total attention is focused on physicality to the extent of eschewing the important aspect of Bhaava or expressiveness. Mask-like faces and robotic movements cannot be termed dance in the way we in the Indian context, have understood dance over centuries. Arguably tenor, tone and direction of dance have undergone changes over time, yet the core values and understanding of significant points in dance have been pillars on which the edifice is built even if its shape and size have seen alterations and course correction. Coming back to the central theme of my article, I was dismayed by frequent complaints of backache, knee problems, slip-disc, neck pain, fatigue and more from my dancers. Some confessed to nurturing old injuries which were not addressed fully and were recurring again. Here is my own story to illustrate how a strong mind can influence the body.

In the year 1974, I was already acknowledged as one of the leading dancers of Bharatanatyam and Odissi. I gave full recitals of either one of the styles or danced both in one evening when four musicians each would be on stage to accompany each style. I had already danced extensively in Europe from the mid-1960s, and by 1974, I had danced in Afghanistan, Iran, Japan, Malaysia, Singapore, Sweden, Germany, France, Switzerland, USSR, Poland, Mongolia, East Germany (before it was reunited with West Germany), USA and Canada. I was now in Bayreuth, Germany in the hallowed town of the father-son composer duo, the Wagners. Coinciding with the annual Wagner Festival of Operas was the International Youth Festival in which I was teaching a three-week dance-workshop to young men and women from some 20 countries. Over weekends, my German fiancé Dr Georg Lechner and I would go to nearby heritage cities of Nürnberg, Würzburg, and Kulmbach to meet with friends while taking in the churches and fortresses of medieval times. On Sunday, 24 August 1974, we drove back from Nuremberg to Bayreuth after spending a delightful day with our painter friend, Herbert Traue. It was past midnight on the autobahn which went through a forested area. At the time Bayreuth was close to the East German and Czech borders so not many people travelled that way. It was drizzling. I was humming a song when I saw a deer head looking at us in the headlights. Brakes were applied suddenly, and the little Volkswagen Beetle keeled over, did three somersaults, throwing me out some 12 to 15 feet away on the hard surface of the autobahn. Those days, cars did not have safety belts. My flight through the air and the impact of the fall had rendered me unconscious. A sprinkle of water and I came to, murmuring, 'I am cold'. My blue Pashmina shawl covered me as I was gently lifted by a male nurse into an ambulance from the nearby town of Pegnitz. One car at a distance of about a kilometre had seen the accident and had called the police from the roadside emergency phone. In Pegnitz General Hospital, doctors awakened at 2 am, came rushing, took X-rays even while I was in great pain, gave me painkillers and recommended that I be taken to Erlangen, city of SIEMENS which had many specialised clinics and hospitals. The ambulance sped off.

My next point in memory, I was lying on a stretcher in the hospital corridor, screaming in pain, the effect of the painkillers having worn off. After two hours, a room was found. The next two days were spent on foam-rubber while Lechner conferred with doctors on the best treatment. X-rays showed the twelfth disc of vertebra smashed to smithereens, with four ribs on the left side broken, and both collar bones broken. By some miracle, the spinal cord was saved by a hair's breadth. Again, as I came out of my stupor, Lechner loomed close to whisper, 'they can operate and insert a steel rod in your back to hold up the spine. Okay?' I believe I just shook my head slightly to indicate 'No'. Lechner conferred with doctors again and said, 'they can only give you Gips, a plaster cast'. I nodded. I feel it was a miracle that I rejected the operation and opted for the plaster cast. What or who could have made that decision? Only the Divine which had more work cut out for me.

I swung between two tables holding up my chin and legs, knee downwards. I sweated profusely. Determined not to scream, I bit my lips as my broken back hanging in space was being swathed in layers of plaster of Paris, cotton wool, and cloth. My fame had spread through German newspapers with banner headlines saying, 'Indian Dance Star seriously injured in road accident'. Doctors and even visitors came to take a peak. Prime Minister Indira Gandhi sent a telegram, 'Keep your chin up. India prays for you.' News of the accident had spread like wildfire in India. Letters, messages and telegrams poured in from known and unknown people. I was a pucca vegetarian and the hospital could offer me only bread-butter and boiled vegetables that I hated. I looked terrible.

On the fourth evening, an Indian lady appeared in my room. Dressed in a lovely silk sari with big round bindi and salt-pepper hair, her presence alone was comforting. She brought out a silver thaali, katoris, spoons, napkin, glass and delicious food! She fed me roti, daal, sabzi, salad, dahi...she had read about me, had met Lechner the previous day and had decided to do this. Her name was Vrinda Swatek. She was married to a Czech national who had met her while in Dehradun as a Prisoner of War (PoW).

Now he worked with SIEMENS in Germany. Thereafter, Vrinda came every day to visit me with a tiffin-carrier. She also brought Hindi and Indian humour with her bright countenance. No other visitor was allowed inside except Lechner and Vrinda. My parents in Bombay wanted to fly in, but were firmly dissuaded by Vrinda on a long-distance call.

The doctors there, soon became admirers. They wanted to hear more about India and Lechner was ever ready to display his knowledge of India where he was serving as Director of the Max Mueller Bhavan, Delhi, before which he had been in Calcutta. Leaving me in Vrinda's care, he had travelled one day back to Bayreuth to collect our things and had taken a room in a hotel near my hospital in Erlangen. I had a full set of gold and ruby jewellery worn during my Bharatanatyam recital which was stolen from the hotel room. This was back in 1974 when Germany's reputation as a nation of hardworking and honest people was at its peak! But that was the least of my worries. I had overheard Dr Vollmar telling Lechner that 'She may be able to walk normally in two years, but not dance'.

I had refused food that evening. 'No appetite' I said. My mind was in a whirl of unknown fears, doubts and ominous signals. Images of my own dancing on prestigious stages of National Theatres and Opera Houses kept flashing before my eyes. Was all this a bad dream? Would I never be able to dance again?

Chapter 14

Pilgrim's Progress in Montreal

Dwijaa's Struggle

From the day after my plastered body—holding up 4 kg weight of the plaster cast—was returned to the room, I also had to wear a rucksack to hold up the broken ribs and allow them to heal. Two male nurses hauled me up gently on my trembling feet. Just standing for a few seconds even though supported by those hefty trained men, I felt dizzy, legs turning to water. The world was spinning madly in my head. From then on, every morning and evening, I was made to stand up, taking one step more, each time. This also gave a boost to my blood circulation and got my stiffened joints to move. Later that week, doctors again conferred with Lechner, advising him to let a chiropractor take care of me who would ultimately decide the right time to cut open the cast and give me adequate treatment. On the fourteenth day after the accident, I was carried on a stretcher to the ambulance in which our luggage had been loaded. Doctors, attendants and many others cheered and waved till the doors closed and we sped on to Frankfurt airport in the company of the two male nurses.

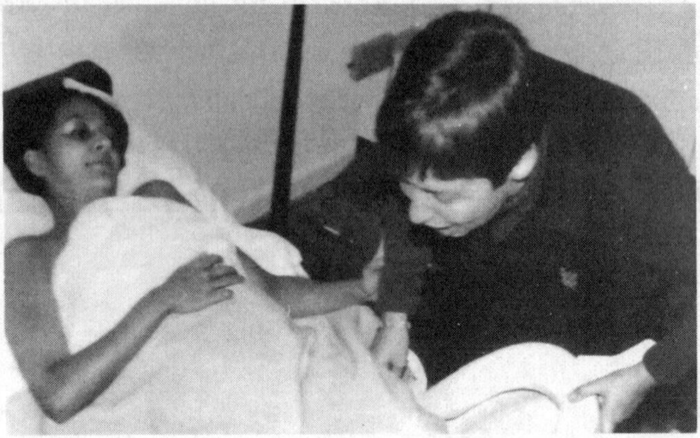

From Star-dancer to helpless, broken being!

The airport clinic was in the basement. I was made to lie down on a bed, given lightly cooked vegetables and asked to rest. Lechner had gone to check us in and tell them to inform us of the time of departure because the ambulance would have to be called to reach me to the aircraft. I stared at the ceiling, slept and suddenly awoke with fright. It was almost time for the flight to take off and we were still in the clinic. Lechner also woke up and ran up to be told that Air Canada had forgotten to switch on the basement speaker while announcing departure! Quickly, I was wheeled out up to the ground-floor exit, wheeled into the waiting ambulance which sped towards the Air Canada flight standing on the tarmac. The ladder was being taken away and the door was closed. The aircraft's turbo-fans were whirring. As my ambulance came to a halt just in front of the nose of the plane, the pilots saw the vehicle, the doors were opened, and the Captain stood with arms firmly crossed at the chest as I was slid down onto the stretcher. I still remember every detail of that dramatic moment when the Captain looked down at me strapped to the stretcher and told Lechner, 'We can't take her. We are not prepared for this'. I was looking up at him as a sacrificial goat might have looked up at her rescuer. Even that did not melt his adamant refusal. In a trice, Lechner whispered to the two male nurses to unstrap and haul me up. I staggered up the 40-odd steps of the ladder helped by the two nurses and greeted the Captain with a dazzling smile and a 'Good afternoon, Captain, thank you!' I still don't know how I did it, but it was almost like climbing Mt Everest without oxygen.

The Captain melted when he heard me talk and despite not having three seats to be able to lie down, he made sure that I was supplied bread, cheese and dessert from the first-class menu. I had to survive a fourteen-hour transatlantic flight with one halt at Shannon, Ireland, in my Economy class seat with two small pillows for support. Visits to the tiny washroom at the back included a lumbering walk, very unlike the nimble-footed gait of a dancer, through a narrow space between seats full of well-endowed passengers, bracing curious glances at my square torso that hid the 4 kg cast under a billowing tanktop. With two pig-tails of black hair and that unbecoming tanktop and skirt teamed with kohl-lined eyes supported by a blond man with green eyes, I overheard several murmurs about my origin. 'She is Mexican.... Italian.... Sicilian...Greek...'

At last, the flight landed at Dorval airport in Montreal, Canada. It was autumn of a rare golden splendour. I had no luxury of a stretcher, just a wheelchair and a long wait for the luggage to be unloaded. Getting me into one of those low-slung, 'Made in America' taxis was an overwhelming task. I could not bend because of the plaster cast from neck to hip. Later, I could laugh at myself re-visualizing the various angles of shove and push by Lechner, taxi driver and wheelchair attendant to pack me into the waiting cab.

On Sherbrook Street West, stands the majestic building Port

Royal in which Lechner had an apartment on the ninth floor with a full glass wall view of the St Lawrence River in the distance and of the busy, fashionable streets of Francophone, Montreal. Hotel Ritz-Carlton was just across the road where Elizabeth Taylor had married Richard Burton for the second time.

It felt good to be back but without any domestic help now, it would be Lechner helped by the German-teacher couple from the Goethe-Institute who would take turns to look after me. There was no question of a bath. I was totally bed-ridden. It took a few hours to unpack and get the well-equipped household functioning. Bernhard and his wife, Hildegard Beutler took turns to spend the day with me while Lechner went to office.

News of my arrival in Canada had done the rounds, and friends wanted to visit but I was in no mood to be looked at with pity. My body had lost colour. I was almost white. Lying on my back, I could move only my fingers and eyes. I went through all the hasta mudras a number of times, and did my eye exercises like a Kathakali dancer. I recreated the accident and the following events only with my hand gestures and eye expressions. Nothing could assuage my feeling of impending doom. Whispers from the living room from where phone calls were made and received, reconfirmed what the German doctors had said, 'She will never dance again!'

Night and day became meaningless. 'Why am I alive? I must die and pray before my last breath that I may be born in India again, learning dancing and fulfilling my unfinished Karma of this birth.' I began denying food. Within two days, I was white as the sheet on which I lay. The room's ceiling became my confidante. My self-deprecations, prayers, questions and taunts were all addressed to that ceiling where they remained looking down at me, mocking me. 'Look at yourself, Dancer! You are a mummy. Don't even dream of dancing. Your life is empty and devoid of joy. Every day, you are a burden on others and yourself. Why are you hanging on?'

Tears ran down my pale, bony cheeks. Visions of my Gurukula-vaasa and of living in the Guru's home to learn dance in Bangalore brought momentary relief. I tried doing mental dance, but the thread would break suddenly, as shooting pains obliterated every other feeling. The only constant refrain in my conscious and subconscious was, 'Why me?'

Then, on the third or fourth day, a Gandhara Buddha appeared,(Gandhara School is the Indo-Hellenic style in sculptures which developed after Alexander's visit to the North-Western areas of present-day Afghanistan and Pakistan). I had visited the famous, now demolished Bamiyan Buddhas in Afghanistan in 1969 when I went with the cultural delegation accompanying then Prime Minister Indira Gandhi. I saw them again in 1971, tall and erect like a king with serene faces and big kind eyes. This Buddha was Dr Pierre Gravel, the famous chiropractor. He had seen me give a lecture-demonstration just a couple of months earlier. The Goethe-Institute staff was so taken

Recovering in Montreal after the accident

by my appearance and fame, that they had insisted on organising a function in their office premises. I was ever-ready to dance. Pierre was invited by the deputy director. Both had found friendship over good food and wine. Now Pierre, who had been vacationing in the Laurentian Mountains about a three-hour drive from Montreal, was informed about my accident. He drove straight to our home.

Later, he confessed that usually he would not have disturbed his well-earned summer holiday for anything, but when he was told it was the Indian dancer whom he had seen a few months ago, he lent his ear. Then, as he heard that she had met with a terrible accident and had broken her back, he dropped his yacht on the lake, his fiancé and cats in the chalet, and drove down. He told me later how profoundly he had been moved by Indian dance that evening. He himself played the violin and regularly attended concerts wherever he travelled. He had seen operas in Milan and Venice. He had heard the greats of Western classical music like Pablo Casals on the cello, Nathan Milstein, Heifetz, Yehudi

My angel Dr Pierre Gravel with wife Myrto,
Montreal, Canada

Menuhin on the violin, Glenn Gould on the piano and Jean-Paul Rampal playing the flute. He had heard opera singers like Luciano Pavarotti and Maria Callas. He was a true music buff.

I only saw a deep gaze from enormously big blue eyes, a mop of curly golden-brown hair and a long French-Canadian nose. Those eyes held mine for a few minutes and were about to drop a tear when he turned away. Lechner and he talked for a while, while I waited to hear his pronouncement. He left and I went back to my self-loathing and despondency. 'What can he do except give sympathy,' I thought. Lechner kept mum but the Beutler couple came as usual and when I refused food for the fourth day in a row, Lechner revealed what Pierre had planned. He had taken my X-rays to study and speak to doctors in Germany, which he had done. It was another week before he reappeared with his own X- ray machine and nurse. He took new X-rays. After another three days, as he stood at the foot of my bed he looked grim. My heart sank. I was trying to touch him with my eyes. There were moments ticking by which were actually my heartbeat going thud-thud in my aching chest.

At last his voice broke the thick silence. 'I am afraid....', he began and paused. Involuntary sobs escaped me, and my eyes welled over. I shut my eyes. This dramatic pause was to give me the kick-start back to life as I learnt later. 'I am afraid you will be able to dance again', his voice caressed my buzzing ears. Was it voice of the Divine?

Chapter 15

Dwijaa

Beginning of Arduous Odyssey of Recuperation

No other sound except my loud screams of relief interrupted my shameless crying. He came to the head of my bed, caressed my hair, held my hand as he led me through the arduous journey back to a life of dance. That scene is even now clearly etched in my crowded memory. 'But it will be hard work, Sonal. You have to promise me to follow everything I say'. I was ready to stand on my head I thought, if he delivered on his promise.

So began the second phase of the torture. He had gauged the exact damage to the vertebra and the discs that needed to be realigned. A low side table of certain height had to be placed under my folded knees for a few minutes at a time, three times a day. It would put pressure on those spots where the discs had moved away and bring them slowly back in alignment, which in turn would release pressure on the nerves pinched by these vagabond discs. I wept helplessly all those painful minutes. I dreaded the sessions. Pierre again appeared the next day with an electric saw to cut a circle around my navel to allow free and deeper breathing. That was a huge relief. Then he again appeared with a long-handled monkey face-back-scratcher to relieve the agonising itch all over my back that was shrouded in plaster cast. That was another huge relief. Each day was lived and experienced in true Zen style, as an existentialist. A supplementary diet of calcium, magnesium, zinc, and more, was added to my daily intake of food and liquids. I was helped in my daily ablutions on the bed itself and I learnt not to feel any shame. A patient has no gender and no age.

I graduated to being propped up in bed. Weeks passed. My brother Anuj was summoned from Bombay to nurse me. He stayed for four months nursing me, driving Lechner to his office, doing the groceries, learning to use the washing machine and a bit of cooking. His Surati (our paternal family tree is from Surat in Gujarat, famous for superb cuisine and witticism) sense of humour helped me laugh and fill my broken ribs with happy oxygen. He was there all through the bitter Montreal winter when some days, the temperature could drop to below zero and

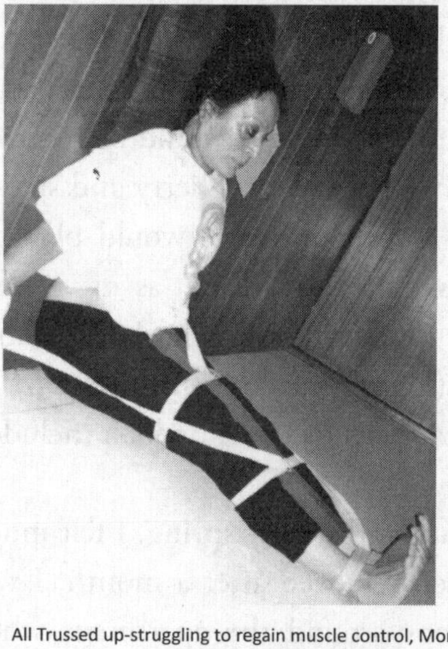

All Trussed up-struggling to regain muscle control, Montreal, Canada (left); Brother Anuj travelled from Bombay to Montreal for four months to take care of me

to minus 35° Celsius at night! He learnt to enjoy wine and cheese, make masala omlettes and generally feel at home in fashionable Montreal. My only regret to date is Lechner denying him a visit to Niagara Falls because it cost USD 100!

Weeks passed and I was helped to walk around the rooms, one room at a time. I saw the familiar streets and Montreal's skyline with new eyes from the windows of the ninth floor apartment. I enjoyed a few moments of sunshine seeping through the glass window. I read entire works of Anais Nin. I re-read Han Suyin and Thomas Mann's 'Buddenbrooks'. I wrote letters to friends in India and rejoiced as their love and prayers reached me a month later by post. Remember, back then, we didn't have email, cellphones, colour TV, STD and ISD codes! Air India did not fly to Montreal so post came via New York or Toronto. Occasionally, I could speak to my parents in Bombay when telephone lines were clear.

Pierre and his lady-friend Myrto visited regularly as did other friends. Initially, Pierre would bring even his X-ray apparatus to the apartment, but later he encouraged me to visit his clinic with help from Lechner and the Beutlers. There, I would be received like a princess with flowers and a glass of dry Sherry and snacks made by Myrto as I was still a vegetarian. He would play his selection of great Western classical music. Then, as my energy sagged, I would be taken home to rest. In hindsight, I don't think I have heard of a doctor's (Pierre was one of the top 10 chiropractors in North America then) treatment which included such heart-warming tactics!

Anuj finally went back to India. By early spring, I felt much stronger. My rucksack had been removed after a month. I was now taking slow, cautious steps around the apartment when Lechner was at Goethe Institute. I noticed the window-dressings and mannequins in the shops across the street change according to the season. Christmas decorations were dazzling. Merry Christmas messages had poured in as did fruit cake and champagne. Encouraged by me, Lechner had gone to Midnight Mass albeit professing atheism. He ate up the New Year goodies as I watched helplessly. Canadian ham cured with maple syrup was world famous as was salmon (fish) from Gaspesie, said to be superior even to what the Norwegians have. I was content in my ignorance about such finer points of Western cuisine. Throughout winter, I was clad in the plastercast and loose shorts. One long loose cardigan and a warm overcoat, muffler and knee-length socks would augment my costume for my visits to Pierre's clinic. I still could not lift my arms to do my hair so whoever was at hand, the weekly cleaning lady, visitors or Lechner, would try to comb my long hair. Most of the time I looked like a strange creature, like something out of Grimm's Fairy Tales or perhaps like Humpty Dumpty.

Pierre was not one to let me off the hook. He prescribed several toe-ankle-knee wiggling and bending exercises which we anyhow did to warm up before Yoga or dance sessions. He asked me to stand in front of a mirror to practice my facial expressions—eyes, eyebrows, nostrils, mouth, and neck. His clinic had also become my workshop where he and the staff buzzed in and out of my corner room as I sipped my goblet of sherry to learn to move my eyebrows, bend my fingers in a simple mudra, and glide my neck, sideways! It provided me with so much fun and mirth just to see them make funny faces and move their derriere instead of the neck. Their eyes went in every direction and their eyebrows refused to budge from their god-given place.

The months passed and as I picked up strength in my legs, arms and mind, I began dreaming. The hours were more profitably spent in mentally going through my repertory of Bharatanatyam and Odissi. In 1973, I had learnt Chhau, the Mayurbhanj style from Orissa, the first woman dancer to do so. One of the great Gurus, Shri Anantacharan Sai known as Kadhubabu had come for one month with a percussionist playing dhol and a muhuri or small shehnai player from Baripada on persuasion from Shri Jivan Pani—the poet-scholar who was later to assume the role of mentor and guide to shape my career. I had watched the Chaitra-Parva Festival in Baripada in 1968 where my father-in-law, Dr Mayadhar Mansingh had taken me. Jivan da, whom I had earlier met in Puri, was then in Baripada, his hometown, and was at hand to explain the finer points. I was fascinated. Later, I argued that Odissi being predominantly lyrical, the Laasya style lacked the masculine Tandava element which I saw in Chhau. There, the Tribhanga became Dharan and the Chowka, the square posture, became more pronounced. The gaits, jumps, pirouettes were spectacular. I had learnt and practised it diligently, spending four hours every morning and two hours every afternoon. Later, in my regular programme in Ashoka Theatre, then the most

Learning Mayurbhanj Chhau wartrail art of Orissa from Guru Anantcharan Sai before the accident, New Delhi 1973

prestigious and coveted venue, I had dedicated the second half to Mayurbhanj Chhau. I had danced in a Berhampuri Paata, the double-twisted silk sari tied as a kutchha or short dhoti. I danced the Salaami, some Uflis and Tapkas which were woven into an item and the difficult Nataraja! There had been astonished silence and then a huge applause. The audience buzzed with surprise. Jivan Pani had introduced this part of the programme explaining briefly the location, genesis and special features of Mayurbhanj Chhau. Mayurbhanj, incidentally was one of the largest princely states before Independence where the royal family was the chief patron and participant in festivals featuring Chhau. After my presentation, several institutions and dancers were inspired to take up Chhau and soon teachers from there were engaged in Delhi.

Chapter 16

Dwijaa

Blessed by the Great Goddess

Unable to leap, sit on my toes or just walk like a dancer, I went through the exercises, steps and compositions in my mind, over and over again. This method was to prove hugely beneficial to me and later to my teaching technique. Unless one 'saves the data' in one's mind-computer and 'accesses' it repeatedly, one can forget even the icon behind which some particular data is hidden.

First bath & hair wash in six months! Georg Lechner combs out clean tresses, Montreal, 1975

One spring weekend morning, Lechner announced a visit to Pierre's clinic which I so looked forward to. We descended the small set of steps and were received by Pierre himself who led me immediately to a traction table in a quiet back room. I lay down, expecting to be put in harness for the mild tractions he had been giving me in earlier visits. As Lechner engaged me in some trivia, Pierre cut through the cast with a soundless electric saw! I went blank. I lay there half-naked, two big pieces of the cast hanging loose on either side. For a long moment, I stared into space. No one spoke. Then I let out a high-pitched wail, sobbing my heart out. 'Is this me? What has happened to me? Why?...' Pierre let me cry, then gently but firmly sat me up and offered me Cognac in a crystal goblet. 'Drink it up,' he said. Between tears and sobs, I swallowed some Courvoisier in one go which stopped my hysteria. As the warmth seeped in, Pierre and Lechner led me next door where a tub full of hot water with aromatic gels washed away all my anguish, pain and dead skin. I was lifted and lowered into the tub, with towel pillows supporting my head. Then, they both set to work to rub fragrant soap and shampoo my tangled hair. That monkey-back-scratcher was artfully employed to relieve every itching spot on my back. To date, it remains the best bath of my life. Fully wrapped in Turkish towels, hair dried with softer towels, I was led to our usual sit-in where Myrto waited with canapes and Dom Perignon champagne. While I drank and ate, Pierre had set up the screen. He ran Walt Disney films 'Ferdinand the Bull', 'Three Little Pigs' and 'Tom & Jerry'. I laughed heartily while Pierre watched me. After an hour of this impromptu picnic, I was dressed in normal clothes which Georg had quietly brought along. I was to go home and lie down on floor on the carpet for an hour. Later in the evening, Pierre and Myrto took us to the best Italian restaurant in town. I had a feast and smoked my favourite Cuban cigar Melia Cohiba, and felt on top of the world.

But then began another round of rehabilitation, equally tortuous and demanding. After a week of feasting and enjoying my cast-less body, Pierre, on an evening visit to us, asked me to stand up and take a dance step. He asked me to remember that first day when I had been introduced to my first dance teacher and the first thing I had learnt. With cocky self-confidence, I got up and took position in front of an expectant audience: Pierre, Myrta, Lechner, the Beutlers, and Martin and Muriel Malina. I took the half-seated Ardha-Mandali position, hands on the waist feeling already like my old self. Then I tried to lift my right foot to strike the first mnemonic syllable Taiya and fell down.

I sat on the floor in utter shock. Everyone in the room was silent. Pierre gently lifted me up. My eyes welled up and I found myself speechless. Even though I was rid of the 4-kg cast, the burden of truth—that I could not lift my leg, let alone take a dance step—felt heavier than anything I had ever known. In that

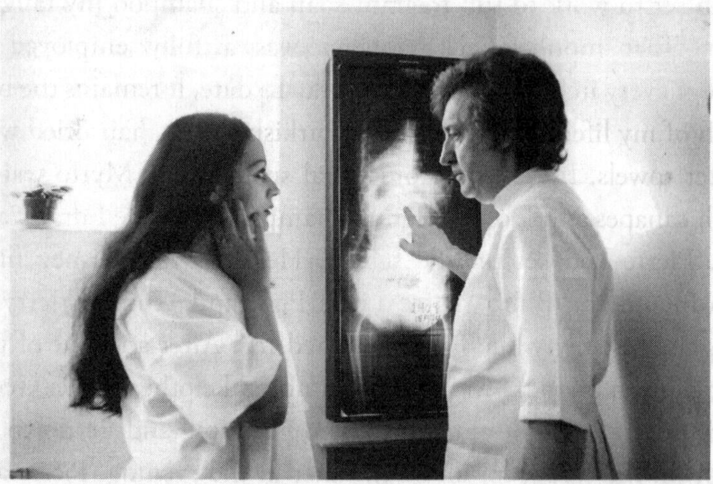

Nature's magic: Pierre showing the natural bone-growth bridging 11th &13th vertabrae in place of 12th which was smashed to smithereens!

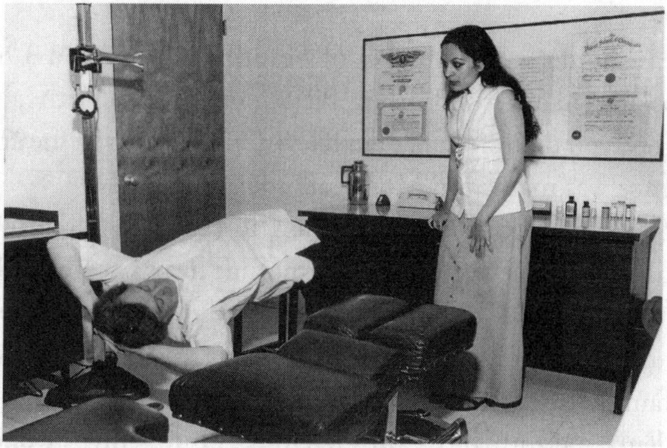

Pierre shows the way!

instant, my cockiness vanished forever. Since then, I have never allowed that self-defeating emotion to enter my mind. Pierre explained how my cramped, unused muscles would need gentle coaxing and repeated practice to bring them to the level of pre-accident strength and suppleness. We worked on a strict regime of exercises where he would supervise me with a stop-watch. Almost like Yoga, nothing was to be done in haste: bending forward and backward, sideways and crosswise—on a stool, on the floor, standing, sitting, lying on the stomach or on the back. Beginning with three-minute slots, he increased it to five minutes and then up to one hour, thrice a day. Slowly, I began to feel the difference. I began practising the basic Adavus of Bharatanatyam and then brought out recordings of my programmes, some of which were on old fashioned tapes winding on a spool. We got an old Grundig recorder and I practised—initially wary of some uninvited cracking sounds from my joints, then gradually pushing the boundaries until I could dance full items.

Dawson College on Sherbrooke St. West invited me to perform. I wore my favourite royal purple-golden border costume and did three items and which got me a standing ovation at the end. At home, a huge basket of beautiful flowers and a box of chocolates had arrived from Pierre and Myrto with a note: 'Hurray, you did it!!' Canadian television interviewed me and my presence was marked in Montreal's social life.

Pierre now gave me permission to travel to India for two months I was able to perform but not lift heavy weights. Then, I was to report back to him. I sent news to my family in Bombay and to friends in Delhi. I flew to Bombay and after a week with my family, I flew off to Delhi. On 4 May, I gave my first post-accident performance in Delhi. Only my wonderful Bharatanatyam musicians, Pandanallur Swaminathan, mridangist K Nagarajan, fluist T Sankaran and vocalist Kamakshi Kuppuswamy were at the airport to receive me. That was the real homecoming, but I was still homeless as I had been most of my life. We drove to Mythili Rajgopal's C-1/48 Shahjehan Road government flat where I had been given shelter since 1973. Daily rehearsals were held in Mythili's living room with kind permission from the ground floor neighbours on whose heads I stomped away each day during my dance practice!

Ashoka Theatre had the reputation of being the most happening venue for dance and music. Cultural advisor to ITDC, Mr Jaspal called Mythili to say that tickets were sold out and the who's who of Delhi were attending. It made no impression on me, as i was immersed in delineating nuances of the deceived Naayika in one of the most difficult, long and demanding Varnams in Bharatanatyam repertory—the Navaragamalika Varnam, a gem in the Pandanallur repertory—to which my Gurus belonged. The Pandanallur style is one of the four major schools of Bharatanatyam.

I danced the full Margam for nearly two-and-a-half hours to a rapt audience and thunderous applause after every item. The

Maharathis of 1975 Delhi's cultural glitterati and celebrities had converged to check whether Sonal could really dance again. Some in the audience saw arcs of light as I danced. Some said they didn't see me, only the dance. Others reported goosebumps and tears all along. Unconscious of all this, I had danced to my heart's content. I was back where I belonged.

An avalanche of invitations followed from all over India and abroad after this recital. As promised, after two months I reported back to Dr Pierre Gravel who took new X-rays and invited Lechner and I to view them. He lit them up, hopped around, did a jig, hugged and kissed me, even shedding a tear while pointing to the place where the twelfth vertebra had been smashed to

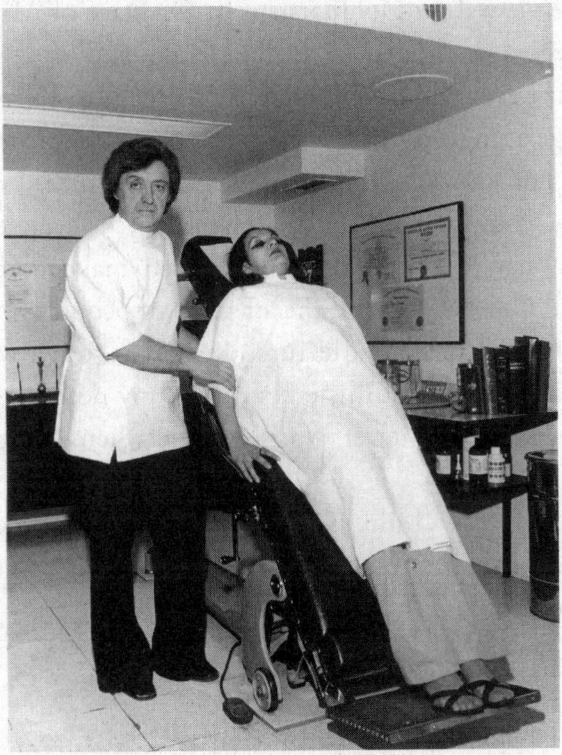

Traction, push-ups, exercise

powder. I could not see any empty space because as Pierre so excitedly said, a new bone—like a bridge—had grown connecting the eleventh and thirteenth vertebrae!

'You demanded and Nature provided,' he said. I gawked. Lechner was confused. There, on the X-ray panel was my own spine! Strong and supple, ready to undertake long journeys, sleepless nights on flights or on train or road, arduous solo recitals and much more. That spine has served me well till now, not only on stage but also in life situations when I have stood up against untruth, injustice and political ostracism.

A few years later, I invited Dr Pierre Gravel and Myrto to India. They met the President and Prime Minister of India and were interviewed on Doordarshan by Dr Dave of AIIMS. They were cheered and feted in Delhi, Jaipur and Bombay. Yet, I wonder if I ever will be able to repay the debt to Pierre who did not charge a single dollar for the miraculous treatment.

I do not know anything else, except to dance. I can't type, work on computers, run the marathon, win gold medals, and I'm not an MBA; nor do I know how to make money. But by God's and Guru's grace and the affection of people everywhere, I am still invited to dance, lecture, do Kathas, teach workshops, write articles and all of this takes care of my needs. As I do not have greed, I have never worried even when going through testing times.

This, my second life, is full of movement and moments of light and laughter. I thank my stars for making me a Dwijaa, twice born!

Chapter 17

Raadha

Years ago, as I sat loudly wondering about Raadha and her fate, the discussion turned to a plethora of folk tales about her. Almost every region in India has its own version of parables, myths, legends and stories about this enigmatic character who has an unshakeable hold over our collective imagination. Centuries and millennia have failed to dim the allure and fascination. Was she a real person, this beloved of the mercurial Krishna? Is she the one mentioned in the Srimad Bhagvat, if not by name, then by allusion? Why is she elevated to be called Krishna's 'Hladini' or 'Allahadini' shakti, a personification of Krishna's power to attract and of his charismatic energy? Why have numerous saints and poets written hymns, poems, songs and verses on her and how do we explain Raadha-ecstasy experienced by Chaitanya, Jayadev, Vidyapati, Chandidas, and Sri Aurobindo among many others?

The more I thought about her, the more I was convinced that there was much more to the lady than being merely Krishna's 'arm candy' as many amongst today's youngsters might call her! Raadha was the epitome of feminine beauty, grace, wisdom and was, at once, shy, bashful and yet adept at playing out the many nuances of love. All this is well known. Arguably, one can rarely find another female character with similar attributes. The curious could then ask how Raadha gained supremacy over Krishna as also over our imagination? Till date, the debate is on: Was Raadha a real woman or a figment of our imagination? Even though she was not a goddess like Devi Parvati or Devi Lakshmi, she has attained the status of one. She was, perhaps, not a living being known to history, yet she lives on in the hearts and minds of savants, philosophers, scholars, poets, dancers, painters, sculptors and, most importantly, in the subconscious of India's spiritual-cultural ethos.

I am not offering a learned paper on Raadha, but rather trying to describe my own relationship with her. I was raised in a Gandhian-Gujarati family in which every form of the Divine was worshipped. We had fun-filled celebrations on Holi, Janmaashtami (Krishna's birthday), Navaratri, Ganesh-Chaturthi and of course, Diwali. Extra holidays on Eid, Christmas, Buddha Jayanti, Mahavir Jayanti, Gandhi Jayanti, and more were most welcome.

At the feet of Beloved: Shree Krishna begging for Raadha's grace

The maximum fun was guaranteed on Janmaashtami as we children of the combined Pakvasa families (cousins, friends, uncles, and aunts) went on 'Govinda Aala Re' rounds around Bombay. In the decades of the 1950s and 1960s, Bombay was nicely manageable. Our Gujarati-medium Fellowship High School on Gowalia Tank also held Govinda celebrations. We enjoyed screaming and helping the boys make a pyramid—only to push them to the ground again and again until finally, out of pity, we girls allowed them to actually reach the earthen pot of white butter and few coins. The boys could eat the butter, but the coins had to be handed over to us girls and woe befell anyone who tried to cheat on us! And then we were picked up by the family for that extended round of the suburbs to cheer, scream, jostle, shove and generally forget the original colour of our mud-and-butter-splattered clothes!

So where was Raadha all this while? Perhaps peeping from a trellised window or from behind a tree? While the Gopis made merry with Krishna and his naughty friends, she was apart—a witness just watching with eyes fixed on Krishna. Countless songs have described these childhood exploits of Krishna in every known language and dialect of India. But so little is heard of Raadha after Krishna left her weeping as Akrura's chariot drove the two brothers, Balaram and Krishna to Mathura to fulfil their destiny. He—the saviour of mankind, as the peerless lover and the greatest teacher of all times—was not to see his beloved Raadha ever again. Now comes the turning point in the narrative of 'My Raadha' as I travel to Dwarka on her trail.

Indian oral and folk literature is replete with stories seemingly contrary to the known narratives set out by our shastras epic and textual traditions. I have been fortunate to hear many such stories which somehow supplemented and complimented the strictly traditional ones. They rounded out the character and filled in the gaps in my perception and comprehension. Once, while working on a new choreography for my solo dance recital, I thought about Aatma—that intangible yet undeniable force which illuminates the darkest of moments. As a close associate and I sat discussing the project, he narrated a simple popular tale about Raadha's visit to Dwarka. She was received with affection by Krishna and with jealous admiration by his queens including Queen Satyabhama.

They always wanted to show her in poor light because Krishna never tired of talking about her in glowing terms. After a while, as they entered the royal garden, Satyabhama hit upon an idea which would, once and for all, settle the issue of who loved Krishna the most. Pointing to a blue water lagoon across which lay a thin bamboo, Satyabhama, with cunning playfulness, asked Raadha if she would accept a challenge to prove her love for the Lord. Innocent Raadha nodded. Krishna, as if warming up to the theme, elaborated the challenge: whoever walked across that bamboo with a water-filled pitcher held on the head without

Take my little frightened boy, Krishna, home—says Nanda to Radha. Opening verse from Shree Gita Govinda by poet Jayadeva, 12th century, Orissa (Miniature Painting)

Without Raadha No Krishna!

supporting it with hand and without faltering or slipping, would have proved intense and true love for him.

Satyabhama smirked and asked Raadha to go first. Raadha merrily skipped across humming a lilting tune and placed the pitcher at Krishna's feet. He now looked at Satyabhama who had tucked in her sari, tightened her hair in a coil and made a mental note of Raadha's speed while crossing the waters. She would do better and prove her supremacy for all time to come. Lifting the pitcher on her head, she threw a coquettish smile at Krishna. With swaying hips, she placed her hands on her ample hips and began her careful journey across the shimmering blue waters. A couple of times, she swayed, a little too much. With total concentration on the pot and bamboo, she tried desperately but could not hold her balance and slipped. With a whoosh and a splash, Satyabhama and her pitcher were seen bobbing in the waters. Servants and maids ran to lend a hand to the queen.

Satyabhama stepped out, dripping wet. With a wilted-lotus face and teary eyes, she sat at Krishna's feet and said, 'I love you more than life. Then how could this happen?' Krishna explained that while she was concentrating only on the pitcher and bamboo, Raadha was immersed in him, and was therefore able to cross without a care in the world. Raadha was Krishna-mayee.

Here ended the folk tale. My vivid imagination took it farther: Raadha did not agree. She turned to Krishna looking him straight in the eye and said, 'No Krishna, it is not so. I am fully immersed in myself, my Aatma, in which I see the entire Creation. I carry the totality of everything that is created within me. Thus, you too, Krishna—as a part of that creation—reside within me. I am Aatma-leen Raadha, the self-immersed Raadha. I am the very personification of Ananda, the Bliss and Ultimate Delight. I am Ananda Roopeshwari.'

Another interesting turning point came with Prof Ramachandra Gandhi, or Ramubhai's, simple one-word challenge. After listening to my narrative, he had a question of how I would tackle this choreography:

'Sonal why don't you bring in Kurukshetra?'

I was stalled in my track of Hurrays and Halellujahs! What on earth could that mean?

'Ha ha ha! Raadha did not visit Kurukshetra, so what is the connection?' I asked in jest.

Ramubhai simply said, 'Find it. Even I don't know, but the word came to me so it is up to you now.'

I had twenty-four hours before blocking the script and starting rehearsals. Early, the next morning, it played out in my half-asleep, stretched out mind. I saw Arjuna look up at Krishna with affectionate admiration, now as a friend. The Gita had been enunciated, Arjuna had seen Vishwaroopa, the cosmic form of Narayana. He had imbibed the attributes of one, whose duty is towards action without attachment to the fruits of that action. He rose, and placing one hand over Krishna's shoulder and asked with a mischievous smile, 'Krishna, from where comes this great Knowledge?' In my dream, Krishna smiled and with a faraway look in his eyes that somehow seemed to light up his entire being, he quietly said, 'From Raadha.'

Chapter 18

Draupadi

In a concerted pre-Diwali clean-up drive, I came across some valuable and wonderful notes written by me for many of my original compositions and choreographies. It had been my habit to write down my thoughts, which often later inspired me to translate them into actual choreography. Also, I had a predilection for composing original music, too. From early on, I was very particular that music should be visual. I insisted that while listening to it, one should be able to visualise the dance and understand the storyline. The mood and situation of the character should reflect in the music. Even then, my insistence on getting at not just the word-meaning, but meaning with nuances and Dhwani—or the unexpressed meaning—would guide me through meandering texts, sub-texts and commentaries aided by my scholar-friends who enjoyed endless hours of debate and discussion with me. Thus, as I offer my Draupadi to you, I have to confess to my own amazement at the deepest level in my subconscious where she still breathes and lives.

In 1994, I stood at the point in my life and career when I was ready to take a quantum leap deeper within myself and effect a

At her Swayamvar, Draupadi and assembled Kings

significant change in my style of working and dancing. Naatya comprises of dance, music and theatre—the only tradition that remained to be tried out. I started from the premise of delight in this work of exploration, trials, search and deeper understanding of characters, situations as well as elements of theatre and dance that could coalesce as a unity. Not for a moment have I worried about the prospect of success or failure. Those terms are not applicable here, for the simple reason that the journey is always more rewarding than the destination. In this case, when the goal is to experience the joy of unraveling the mysterious processes of creativity and the delight of getting to know those magnificent yet very human characters, the whole exercise becomes meditative. May Draupadi be the beginning of a new phase of greater respect and autonomy for women.

Draupadi Through My Eyes

Perceptions are highly subjective because they emanate from an individual point of view, coloured by the psychology and physicality of the perceiver. Thus, Draupadi was seen through

Vyasa's eyes and described through the prismatic perceptions of the Pandavas, the Kauravas and Krishna. Except for Krishna, all men saw her in parts and not in totality. This is the eternal paradox of the fullness of beings like Krishna and Draupadi whose essence eludes most of us and can only be experienced in parts. She is Prakriti, the cosmic principle of creation and dissolution. She is Kaali, the dark Goddess who plays with time, creating it and devouring it. She is the concept of Karma or

Flames of Fair! That hair by which Darupadi was dragged to the Kaurava Court

Action incarnate; Draupadi is also every woman.

I have been her companion since my childhood. She fascinated me all along my adolescence and youth. Then she began to occupy centre-stage in my psyche and for the past five years, demanded 'abhivyakti'—active attention and delineation.

I am looking at Draupadi from the inside out, not the other way round. All the narratives and descriptions about her do not tell me about those poignant moments in her life—and there were many—when she must have reacted sharply, forcefully or shyly; a time when she must have made her stand clear to one and all and still maintained her dignity and self-respect in the face of the unspeakable outrage against her persona.

I am thinking of the new bride—shy, playful, young and beautiful, perhaps dreamy—looking forward to a warm, loving embrace from the handsome, manly Arjuna whom she had garlanded at the swayamvara. She was not free to choose her husband according to her will like Rukmini or Indumati; instead, like Sita, she was bound to marry the man who would match up

Mother Kunti orders the five Pandava brothers to marry Draupadi

to the difficult conditions set by her father. This was not a swayamvara in the true sense. Following him out of the royal palace and through the city to the far-away hut of a potter, where the five brothers lived with their mother, Kunti and are staying incognito, she was confronted by the rude shock of a strange welcome to her new home. In response to Arjuna's gleeful announcement, 'See, what I have brought today', came his mother Kunti's reply from inside the hut: 'Distribute it equally among your brothers.'

We are told by Sage Veda Vyaasa, author of the epic *Mahabharata* that as Kunti came out and saw Draupadi and Arjuna with the victory garland around his neck, she immediately regretted her words. Yet, as her words could not be retrieved, she asked the eldest, Yudhishthira, to find a way to accommodate her command which would be commensurate with Dharma, code of ethics.

My own view was that leaving Arjuna and Bheema to keep off the belligerent kings, the other three brothers hurried away to give the news to their mother. Yudhishthira might have coloured his information with a tinge of envy (because despite being the eldest, he was nowhere in the picture). The intelligent mother must have understood the nuances and said what she did later in full knowledge of the situation, maybe as a ploy to preserve emotional and physical unity among the five Pandavas. So Draupadi is ordered by the mother-in-law to be the common wife of all five men. I wonder if any woman would accept such a situation?

Draupadi's sense of disbelief, shock and distaste at the callous treatment and total disregard for her own emotions and dignity finds no place in the Mahabharata. This is one of the poignant moments in her life when she turns away, hesitates and finally accepts her destiny, with grace. The elongation of that moment was my concern.

Her relationship and friendship with Krishna filled me with a sense of envy. She is his only friend, the rest were either wives, devotees or admirers. But in this case there is a perfect understanding and trust between them.

They must have enjoyed each other's company, indulged in witty conversation and repartees as Draupadi was more than a match even for Krishna. Her child-like innocence and purity is not underlined in the popular interpretations of her character.

Anyone who enjoyed Krishna's unstinted admiration and whose words merited immediate action by him deserved my unbound and awestruck devotion.

Her own sense of duty and responsibility to the family she is married into does not allow her to accept any compromises, even when the eldest among her husbands with the title of 'Dharmaraja' or Master of the Code of Correct Ethics of Life, is willing time and again to let things be. This paragon of virtue, Yudhishthira—a gambler and a weak-minded man—jeopardises not only her life but also those of his brothers. He stakes her in the game of dice even after losing his own freedom and that of his brothers when he had lost the right to do so. When Draupadi questions the ethics and morality of such a game and conduct, no one has the answer. All that she gets is undiluted scorn from the Kauravas, a weak-kneed sermon from Bheeshma and stony silence from Yudhishthira! An intelligent woman capable of arguing her case and showing up chinks in male logic proves too much even today, so to whom could Draupadi turn to for help, then?

The public disrobement of Draupadi is a chapter that has created trauma and repercussions over centuries—a shameful event of cosmic dimensions. The denudation of Earth-Nature-

Prakriti-Draupadi causes holocausts in every age and aeon.

There are a myriad dimensions to Draupadi's persona and story; she is larger than life yet very much a ripple in the perennial river of life. She reflects universal womanhood—proud, dignified, unbending, magnanimous, articulate and uncompromising.

She has five names, each revealing a grand dimension of her unusual persona.

Yaagyaseni: She who is born from Yagnya, the sacrificial fire. King Drupada prayed for progeny from the God of Fire, Agni to avenge insults by an erstwhile friend, Guru Drona. He received two: Dhrushtadyumna, who was to behead Drona during the great war at Kurukshetra, and a daughter, who was to be the main female protagonist of the epic Mahabharata.

Krishnaa: She arose from the fire, a fully formed woman, her skin swarthy and tinged like a blue lotus. Her long, dark, silky, thick, curly hair flowed beyond her knees. Her given name, therefore, was Krishnaa, the Dark ONE, just like her friend, Krishna. The name has another meaning too—from the root word in Sanskrit "karshan", to attract and to be bewitched. She, like Krishna, was the centre of attraction wherever she went. Her beauty, stance, posture, gestures and glances all added up to a woman of infinite variety that confused and confounded the best pundits.

Paanchaali: Paanchal was an important and powerful kingdom. As the princess of Panchal, she was known as Paanchaali.

Mahabhaarati: The adjective depicts her as the heroine of the epic Mahabharata. It also means the great woman of the country known as Bharat. Bhaarati is one of the many synonyms for the goddess of wisdom, learning, knowledge and the arts—Saraswati. Our heroine possessed all these attributes which made her a superior female icon.

Draupadi: In ancient India, persons were known also by the lineage of their parents, for instance, Karana was called Raadheya, son of Raadha; Krishna as Vaasudeva, son of Vasudeva; Bheeshma as Gaangeya, son of Gangaa; Raama as Raghav, from the lineage of Raghu; Sita as Jaanaki, daughter of Janaka, or as Mythili, princess of Mithila. Thus, as the daughter of Drupada, she is Draupadi.

Dru or druma means tree and pada means landmass. Hence, Drupada would mean a forested landmass full of trees and vegetation. Draupadi, then symbolises Nature or Prakriti, and when dishonoured and disrobed, cataclysmic and violent events take place. The wrath of Nature's fury befalls all who do not respect her.

Fire and blood play a significant role in her life. Born from fire, she has a fiery temperament which does not brook nonsense from anyone. She is pulled by her long, curly, flame-like hair by Dushassana while she is menstruating. Duryodhana pulled up his Dhoti to expose his left upper thigh and asked Draupadi to sit there as a wife or mistress would. This elicited terrible vow from the second Pandava brother, Bheema. With a roar he declared, he would break that thigh of shameless Duryodhana. Her one unstitched wrap-around is soiled and bloody. As Dushassana tries to pull it off, Bheema, vows to wrench off those evil hands which dishonoured Draupadi. As the single cloth covering Draupadi was being pulled off, she tried to stop it by holding the cloth with all her strength, but to no avail. About to be completely exposed she thought of Shri Krishna and raised one arm upwards in supplication. As the cloth was about to come off, Draupadi raised the other arm, now letting go of the cloth. It is said that in a split second that cloth became unending. The more it was pulled the longer it became. Dushaasana fell down, fatigued and defeated. Draupadi stood regally offering gratitude to Shri Krishna. In that total silence, each person present in that Court must have felt the divine presence. She vows to leave her entangled hair open until she can wash them with the blood of Dushassana.

In my Draupadi solo dance-theatre, I went through all these emotions and situations. Her anguish and pain became mine. Her disappointment at Kunti's faked surprise was felt by me. I mentally challenged many Yudhishthiras and Bheeshmas to answer every woman's burning questions. What was true in the times of Veda Vyasa was also happening in 1994 when Draupadi was premiered at Delhi, and continues till date not only in India but all over the world.

Let the life of Draupadi be a warning that when Prakriti, the Ultimate Feminine decides to punish, there will be no refuge, no succour and no end to destruction.

Chapter 19

When the Gods Meet

Lessons for Humans are Learnt

Gods speak to us in many ways and in many languages. If our antennas are tuned and minds are open, we catch those messages in sharp clarity. In over sixty years of an active, professional dancing and teaching career, I have benefitted immensely from an attitude of keen humility and an eagerness to receive. Therefore, when ideas drop in my lap like ripe fruit, I pick up one, savour and share it.

Fight between Krishna & cobra king Kaaliya

Sutradhaar-who holds and knits the stories together(1)

Greece and India have intrinsic cultural links going back at least two millennia and more. The Silk Route from India perhaps did not touch Greece, but Alexander touched the Indian subcontinent in many more ways than just a military one. Indo-Hellenic influences imbued art and culture in India. Even the Indian sari is an echo of the Hellenic toga (unstitched long cloth)! I was fascinated by Greek mythology and its parallels to our own myths with gods, goddesses, titans, demons, goblins and humans. Interaction between them went deeper into the collective civilisational psychology and mores.

I selected popular myths from them to create a tapestry of the many emotions, through legends about Krishna, Shiva and Parvati, and of Vishnu as Mohini, the Divine enchantress. From the Greek myths, I selected the legends of Psyche and Eros, Zeus and Europa, Uranus and Gaiia.

While it was a great experience to invite the gods to visit, they demanded my total attention and detailing of every turn and twist in their stories. So, I set to work, discussing how they would want to appear. That is how the pieces were formulated with me as the Sutradhaar knitting the different narratives together. I edited specially created music by the hugely talented husband-wife duo Shubhendra and Saskia Rao playing on sitar and cello, respectively, along with their team of ace musicians. The Mohini-Bhasmasura episode was created by the well-known French vocalist and musician, Ariane Gray Hubert. I hugely enjoyed this responsibility because almost half of the choreography was visualised during the process. As I wrote my Sutradhaar commentary in long hand in the studio before recording, the final piece fell into place. I was that one character in every episode who saw, predicted and knew the outcome.

The Sutradhar's Commentary:

Krishna-Kaaliya (Indian)

I am Sumati, chief queen of Kaaliya, King of the Cobras. When we reached this beautiful, verdant, lush spot on the banks of the river Yamunaa, we decided to make this our home. Slowly the cobra poison killed all including birds, animals and humans. I tried to convince my husband to move to a place that was not inhabited, but he would not listen. Then, one day, I heard a loud splash in the river near where I was, and saw a dark-complexioned, charming boy swimming effortlessly towards my husband who lay quietly in the deep waters. Before I could warn the boy to go away, my husband had woken up. Furious at this intrusion, he lunged at the boy and the fight began. The other queens and I watched helplessly as we saw our husband, the great king Cobra Kaaliya, being defeated and trampled upon. That aura of light—that dark boy—was dancing on the thousand hoods of Kaaliya! Well, such is the fate of wickedness: it is always humbled in the end. That dark apparition, Krishna, did not kill my husband even after defeating him but just ordered him and all of us to go and live in the deep ocean. I bow to that epitome of compassion, Krishna.

Psyche and Eros (Greek)

My sister, Psyche, is the best-looking among us sisters but see what happened to her.

Aphrodite, the Goddess of Beauty herself, became so jealous of Psyche that she sent her son Eros to pierce her with an arrow of love so that she would fall in love with whoever she saw first, a dwarf or a donkey, and thus be ridiculed. Eros saw a sleeping Psyche. So mesmerized with her beauty was he, that his arrow of love poked him instead. He fell hopelessly in love with our sister. Later we asked Psyche about her new mood of exhilaration and that bulge on her stomach!

Who was that?

A beast or a demon?

She lifted the lamp to his face that very night and sighed with joyous relief. But alas, a hot drop of oil fell on sleeping Eros's

Greek Myth of unfulfilled love of Psyche for Eros

forehead. He awoke startled, dismayed by this open admission of doubt and distrust. He left her weeping, never to return. Psyche became Goddess of the Soul, forever yearning and repenting. Oh! The cruel fate of Doubting Damsels!

Mohini-Bhasmasura (Indian)

I am worshipped in all the worlds as Lakshmi, Goddess of Beauty and Prosperity. I enjoy my husband Vishnu's undivided attention. Yet he disappears in a moment as he did just a while ago, leaving me to find out what happened. That my husband's sister Parvati is married to Shiva who is also called Bholanath is well known. Shiva is easily pleased and grants boons to Gods, humans and the anti-Gods alike. He did this to the Asura-King, who asked, 'May all and everything on which I place my right hand, burn to ashes immediately!' The boon was granted and Asura decided to try this out on Shiva, himself. He ran after Shiva, who ran from the

Sutradhaar-who holds and knits the stories together(2)

Asura. This is when Vishnu appeared as Mohini, the Enchantress and at once, the Asura was distracted. Bewitched by Mohini's beauty, he proposed love and marriage. Mohini invited him to a dance competition, and declared that if he won, she would be his beloved. Now, as I watched intrigued by the scene unfolding before my eyes, I saw clever moves by Mohini which compelled the Asura to place his right hand on his head. In a trice, he was burnt to ashes! So, I learnt an invaluable lesson— one should not indulge in evil ambitions.

Europa and Zeus (Greek)

Europa & Zeus

My dearest friend, Europa is the comely and charming daughter of Agenor, King of Tyre. That day, as we were dancing, playing music and making merry on the seashore of the bluest waters one had ever seen, a strange thing happened. A gorgeous virile white Bull with golden horns appeared in our midst. Europa, playful and ever curious, mounted the Bull and before we knew what was happening, they disappeared. We looked for her high and low but couldn't find her or the Bull, could not even find his hoofmarks! Many years later, I met her. She was more charming than ever before. She told me her story: her lover was Zeus, the King of Gods, who in the form of a Bull had galloped off to a flowering bower with her riding on his back. Then their love story unfolded as he lay her down and made passionate love. She introduced me to her children, cherubic girls and boys, adorable and angelic. The joys of love are many. I wondered when I would meet my Zeus.

Divine Marriages (Indian and Greek)

I am very busy. It is my daughter Parvati's wedding day. Soon I will be summoned to receive the bridegroom, Shiva and his party of gods and goblins. I hope he will be appropriately dressed as a bridegroom should be.

We have also made lavish arrangements to receive our divine guests, the Gods and demi-Gods, Apsaras and Yakshas, musicians,

Greek Myth of Marriage of Sky-God Zeus & Earth-Goddess Gaia

Marriage of Shiva & Parvati

dancers and scholars. My special attention is given to arrangements made for the wedding party of our friends Uranus, the Sky God and Gaiia, the Earth Goddess from faraway lands.

They will soon arrive with their entourage.

What a joyous occasion this is! And what a superb coincidence that two divine pairs will be united in marriage. These are rare moments of cosmic conjunctions, moments of divine blessings and grace. Be blessed. May the Divine protect you. May you all experience beatitude.

Kalyaanamastu – कल्याणमस्तु
Shubhamastu – शुभमस्तु
Mangalamastu – मंगलमस्तु

What attracted me to these myths was the eternal messages they carry. If Krishna forgave Kaaliya because of his surrender and admission of wrong-doing, Vishnu did not spare the anti-God Bhasmasura who wanted to test the boon given by Shiva on Shiva, himself! So Bhasmasura had to pay the price by using his own device and burned to ashes. His arrogance and ignorance led him to his own fatal end. In the two Greek episodes, I wanted to highlight the triumph of love and trust between Europa and Zeus and the sad fate of Psyche precisely because she did not trust her love. The last episode was so breath-taking with its splendour and joint wedding ceremonies that everywhere, the audience would stand up bursting into loud rounds of applause. Later, many confessed to tears and choked throats. I can only say, it is bound to happen, When the Gods Meet!

Chapter 20

Same Krishna, Differing Perceptions

The kaleidoscope of life offers different designs using the same pieces which realign with the flick of a wrist to present completely different formations. In my childhood, I had great fascination for this simple device. For endless moments, the kaleidoscope held my attention until my eyes would start watering. It was nothing short of magic and that magic happened with just a flick of my own wrist! That is how dance views life—altering the images with unbelievable simplicity and facility to offer a new angle, a new perception to the deja vu. This is more easily seen in the dance forms of India in which the element of nritya or abhinaya is significant and important. To communicate ideas through the body, by using every possible limb including those minute features on the face like the eyebrows, eyes, nostrils and lips, the Indian dancer is at ease with the body. Every limb, posture, gait, shrug, every turn of the neck and unfurling of fingers suggests an idea or an emotion. This is a unique art which is being given short shrift in favour of group dancing. But my focus here is on the magic of Abhinaya and how innumerable perceptions for a single moment can be offered.

To illustrate this, I offer the popular incident from *Shrimadbhagavat*, biography of the divine human Shri Krishna. Although born to Princess Devaki and the clan chief, Vasudeva, Krishna grew up among cowherds in Gokul and Vrindavan on the banks of the river Yamunaa. As the living incarnation of the great God Shri Vishnu, his mission in life was to re-establish Dharma for which he would annihilate the dark demonic forces prevalent at the time.

Princess Devaki's cousin brother was the evil king Kamsa, king of Mathura whose kingdom included Gokul, Vrindavan, and many other villages. According to divine prediction, Devaki's eighth child (Krishna) would be the nemesis of Kamsa. The following incident takes place when, at the royal invitation, Shri Krishna and his elder brother Balarama enter the city gates of Mathura. Kamsa's evil design to murder Krishna was no secret. In a strange welcome, the notorious elephant Kuvalayapeeda was unleashed after being heavily intoxicated. The brothers beat him down to pulp as he tried to crush them. Next, was an open challenge to wrestle with two gigantic wrestlers, Chanoor and Mushthi. They planted themselves before the two adolescent boys in a scene reminiscent of a mountainous genie looming large over two tiny creatures, almost like a Lilliputian scenario. As the signal was given and action was about to begin, the magical moment is captured in a four-line Sanskrit shloka by poet Lilashuka in his anthology, Krishna-Karnaamritam (chanting Krshna's name is like nectar for the ear). I was taught this for my 1961 Arangetram—my first stage performance for which I was coached by my Bharatanatyam dance guru Prof U S Krishna Rao in Bangalore. The choreography was simple with four different ways to depict each line. Even so, it made an impact on the elite audience including the late Maharaja of Mysore, Jayachamaraja Wodeyar, a scholar-poet and musician.

So it has been all these past decades, experiencing the interplay between yogic focus and a variety of perceptions. I found the same interplay in this short Sanskrit text by poet Lilashuka.

मल्लै: शैलेन्द्र कल्प: । शिशु: इतरजनै: । पुष्पचापो अंगनाभि: ।।
गोपस्तु प्राकृतात्मा। दिविं कुळीशभृता। विश्वकायो अप्रमेय: ।
क्रुद्धः कंसेन कालो भयचकित दृशा। योगिभिर्ध्येयमूर्ति: ।
दृष्टो रंगावतारे हरि: अमरगणानंदकृत् । पातु: युष्मान् ।।

In later years, I added a description of the great event describing joyous activities of the citizens of Mathura in anticipation of Krishna's arrival. Women sprinkled water to settle the dust, cleaned doorways and made colourful Rangoli with geometrical designs of flower petals or coloured powder. Children hung torans or flower buntings on pillars and doorways. Men called upon each other to get ready with instruments.

Each of these activities were danced to different rhythms and melodies because even excitement has different levels and rhythms! For children, I used a playful melody in Tishra-gati, in quick time-units of three beats. For women, I used sweet, slow melody in seven beats, and for men, it was just percussion in five beats. It worked well in denoting the general atmosphere of eagerness in Mathura. Then, I turned to show Krishna and Balarama arriving in a chariot with Kamsa's messenger, Akrura. They alight at Mathura's main gate and start walking inside. Balarama is older and heavier and walks with cocky steps looking straight ahead, while I show Krishna in the Natawari gait of a graceful dancer who looks at people with a smile and greets them with polite salutation—the Namaskar. I alternated between depicting Krishna and the onlookers, whose fascination for him was difficult to convey through posture alone; the face too played a vital role in expressing this collective attraction.

Lilashuka describes the scene through the eyes of different sections of onlookers. He gauges their innermost emotions. He depicts the arena as the two handsome young boys confront the wrestlers and the verse as it explodes from his own awe-struck pen:

Mallaih Shailendra Kalpah

(मल्लै: शैलेन्द्र कल्प:)

As the power-drunk Mallas—wrestlers—lumbered into the arena, confident of knocking the two boys down in a trice and kneading them to pulp as ordered by the king, they looked down pityingly from the impressive height of their own iron-strong tall body; but what they saw instead were two towering, mountain-like figures. Was this a dream or sorcery? Their jaws dropped, eyes almost popping out of their sockets. The scene was interpreted with a show of arrogant strength of the wrestlers who would usually make a great show of their prowess to the cheering crowd. But here the crowds didn't cheer them. Then they looked down at the boys. My whole posture of arrogant tallness changed to disbelief as I fell on my knees, eyes slowly rolling upwards and outwards as if scaling the tallest peak of the Himalaya. The body shrank and shivered in fear, with pupils dilated, arms hanging listlessly and mouth open wide as if to expel fear. It was an expression of utter surprise and disbelief merging with shock. The blood-thirsty wrestlers seemed to see huge mountains and not just boys.

Shishuhu Itarajanaih

(शिशु: इतरजनै:)

The assembled citizens looked at the boys with deep affection as if they were little children—their own little ones.

मल्लै: शैलेन्द्र कल्प: । शिशु: इतरजनै: ।
To the wrestlers, the boy seemed like a huge mountain. To onlookers, he was an adorable child

Pushpachapo Anganaabhih
(पुष्पचापो अंगनाभि:)

But what of the womenfolk? Each one was filled with passion for that Blue Lotus—the very embodiment of Kamadeva, God of Love and desire, who shoots five flowery arrows of love from a bow of fragrant flowers. While conveying this delicate situation, I had brought into play the many postures of love-struck women and the effect of those five arrows on them. Kamadeva has many synonyms, which while dancing, added to the density of passion: Ananga (bodiless), rati-pati (Rati's husband, who presides over passionate-love-play), manmatha (one who churns up emotions and the mind), pancha-bana (having five arrows ready to be shot at poor unsuspecting victims), smara (one who jolts memory of

पुष्पचापो अंगनाभि:
Young women were smitten by his beauty rivaling Kamadev

love), pushpa-chapa (holding a flower-bedecked bow) and of course Kamadeva (God of Desire).

Anganaa means youthful charming women just like other synonyms Vanita, Lalana, Ramani, and Vamaa. I could take up different languorous postures—sitting, half-seated, standing; women smitten to the core by the charms of Krishna. All at once, I became a naturalist and environmentalist by bringing the five flowers to the notice of the audience, many of whom may not have ever seen some of those lovely flowers. As the effect of the arrows was shown, each viewer became the victim! I was told by friends how they involuntarily wiped their brow and placed a hand on the throat just as I was performing on stage!

Then I depicted the five arrows because they are fashioned from five different flowers and are shot at different parts of the body causing varying effects. I present one such scene here:

Arvind: White Lotus arrow aimed at the bosom or vaksha which makes the woman lose control over her emotions. This condition is known as being Unmatta.

Ashoka: This is the mildly fragrant orange flower which grows in round bunches. In the Ramayana, Devi Sita was confined within a grove of Ashoka trees. This arrow is aimed at the lower lip or adhara that causes taapa or intense sweating due to the heat of passion.

Amra-manjari: Arrow of aromatic mango flowers which is aimed at the forehead or lalaat. It causes dryness in the mouth.

Navamallika: This is an arrow of delicate and fragrant, new jasmine flowers aimed at the eyes which can cause a loss of motivation to move, known as sthambhan. The victim stands, as if nailed to the spot.

Neelotpala: A blue lotus arrow is aimed at the entire body. It causes bewitchment and enchantment.

All the flowers are seasonal in India. They are fragrant, aromatic, delicate, beautiful and colourful and are found in abundance if only we have the time and inclination to see them blooming around us.

Gopastu Praakrtaatmaa

गोपस्तु प्राकृतात्मा।

The fun-loving cowherd boys of Gokul-Vrindavan, who had also reached Mathura to be with their dearest buddy, saw Krishna as they always did—a friend and a cowherd boy, just like themselves.

गोपस्तु प्राकृतात्मा
To cowherds he was one of them

Divim Kulishabhrtaa Vishvakaayo Aprameyah

दिविं कुळीशभृता विश्वकायो अप्रमेय:

But to Indra, chief of the heavenly hosts high up in the sky, Krishna appeared to wrap the universe within himself; it was Krishna who was beyond perceptions and premises.

दिविं कुळीशभृता। विश्वकायो अप्रमेय:
To Indra in high heaven, he appeared as the imminent, ever expanding Universe

Kruddhah Kamsena Kaalo Bhayachakitaa Drshaa

क्रुद्धः कंसेन कालो भयचकित दृशा

That very moment, to a frightened Kamsa, Krishna appeared as Death personified.

क्रुद्धः कंसेन कालो भयचकित दृशा
Kamsa's fury transformed into fear as he saw Death approaching

Yogibhirdhyeyamoortih

योगिभिर्ध्येयमूर्तिः

All the yogic energies of seers and seekers were focused on him. He was the very reason for their deep meditation, and the central image of their Dhyana.

योगिभिर्ध्येयमूर्तिः
He was the one for whom Yogis meditated

Drshto Rangaavataare Harih

दृष्टो रंगावतारे हरिः

He is Hari, because he removes all negativity. "Harati" is a verb in Sanskrit. He chooses to make this world his stage, for his many manifestations.

दृष्टो रंगावतारे हरिः अमरगणानंदकृत् पातुः युष्मान्
May Hari protect you whose cosmic playfulness brings joy even to the Immortal Ones.

Amaraganaanamdakrit

अमरगणानंदकृत्

He grants bliss even to the Immortal Ones.

Paatuh Yushmaan

पातु: युष्मान् ।

May he protect you with this benediction.

Let me invoke the manifestations which we can see with our eyes as well as those which can only be perceived with our inner eyes and a prayer for the good of all.

Chapter 21

Dance of Enlightenment

How an innocuous query can shake one awake!

Many years ago on one of my dance tours, I was offering Nritya-Seva, a form of worship through dance at the ancient temple of Guruvayoor, where the presiding deity, an adolescent Krishna, seemed to wink at me. My group of musicians and I had driven into Trichur after that performance. There were two lecture demonstrations in colleges the next morning and evening as I usually liked to combine these with regular recitals. At the end of my second lecture-demonstration, there was a lively and humorous Q&A session. After the vote of thanks, it was time to leave for the railway station to travel further to Cochin to catch my flight back to Delhi. As I made to get off the dais, a simple lady draped in a fawn-coloured nylon sari rose to ask a question. I was in a hurry, but could not refuse. Her question stumped me: 'Why do compositions on which you dance and sing always refer to the male gods as the beloved or lover? Is there anywhere a male poet who addresses a goddess thus?' I was speechless. Gathering my wits, I was able to express my ignorance on the matter but promised to do research on the topic. I thanked her profusely for shaking me awake from my comfortable zone of performances and routine acclaim and admiration.

After returning to Delhi, I looked at my repertory both in Bharatanatyam and Odissi styles of dance which use beautiful musical compositions by saints and poets, mostly male. At the time, I must have had fifty or sixty compositions in Bharatanatyam and an equal number in Odissi (at present, my Odissi repertory consists of 300 plus). Somewhere, hope lurked within me, of finding at least one song—Varnam, Padam, Keertanan Javali, Geet, Janana, Champu—in which a goddess was the beloved of the male poet, composer or saint. Disappointment made me ask my mentor-guide Shri Jivan Pani about my dilemma. He too was stumped but promised to think and research. Sure enough, after one week, my phone rang at 11 pm. 'Eureka!' he shouted. We met the next day and discussed the topic for hours. I was in tears of gratitude and joy. Jivanda had found the answer in Chariyaa-Geeti of the Vajrayaan Buddhist texts. He had brought four or five of those written in his own hand, copied from the original text! I can still experience that excitement, that rush of blood to my head. Some of these were re-transcribed in Devanagari script from one of the languages of Tibet. While Sanskrit was the language of the Court and of the educated, Prakrit was the local lingo. Thus, we have Odiya Praakrit, Maraathi Praakrit, Gujaraati Praakrit and so on. We selected three of those for our purpose of countering the Trichur lady's conscience-raising question. In two of them, the Araadhya is female—the one sought after in worship, the fulfiller of spiritual aspirations. She is the Ultimate.

Chariyas are songs of the Siddhas, taken from India to Tibet in the centuries following Guru Padma Sambhava's travel to Tibet in seventh century AD. These are also known as Chhaya-Geeti because the textual content hides many layers of metaphors and meanings, deeply moving insights in the realm of metaphysics, tantra and Buddhist philosophy. Later, the lyrics were set to raagas drawn from the Sangeet-Ratnakar, the 13th-century text on music. One of them, Shoonya-Mahari—Dancer in the Living Void—is a dialogue between Sabari, the tantric painting symbolising life energy or the Supreme Shakti which lies coiled in the void, the infinitesimal space within the spinal cord, and the Sabara youth representing the body entwined around the axis mundi or the spinal cord. The Sabaras are one of the oldest tribes on the Indian subcontinent residing in mountainous and thickly forested regions of western Orissa. Among those who know about left-handed Tantra practices, Saabara-tantra is supposed to be the most mysterious and difficult to counter. This song, as well as Dombi, the second song in which a young Brahmin youth is the seeker, gave me new insights about imagery and connections between everything tangible and intangible, Hindu and Buddhist, mega and mini. Simply put, one remains a life-long seeker, birth after birth. I shall not elaborate upon the

Ecstacy on Ashtapath, dancing for Nataraja & Nateshwari in front of Mt. kailas, 2006

content of the Chariyas except to say that these geetis or songs were the outpourings of 16 Siddhas of Vajraayana Buddhism. Some readers may be acquainted with the name Milarepa whose vivid image of being seated with one hand cupping the ear as if listening to the music of the spheres is often found in the markets of Nepal, Bhutan and among Buddhist settlements in India.

Among the three songs, two are by Kanpa or Kanhapa, originally Krishnapada, an Oriya by birth. They are Rajahamsa-chariya and Dombi. We could not determine the author of Shoonya-Mahari or Sabari. We also worked on the musical framework of those Raagas as a prelude to the structure of the text without which the essence would not emerge like fragrance from a flower.

Rajahamsa means the Royal Swan, a reference to the mythical swans from Mansarovar. Roughly translated, it would mean Lake of the Mind. The text exhorts a seeker to sit at the feet of the Guru and listen carefully to the upadesha by the end of which the seeker would be able to drink only the milk or essence, leaving the residue water, a metaphor for unnecessary thoughts, habits, and practices. We set the text in three Raagas which had Hamsa i.e. Swan in their names, namely Hamsanaraayani, Hamsaanandi and Hamsadhwani. Shoonya-Mahari was to be sung in Vaaradi and Dombi in Desakhya. The text and Raagas melted into each other so beautifully that I burst into tears while singing and performing these, even today.

In 1993, I was at the Tibetan Theatre Institute, in McLeod Ganj, Dharamshala. My neck was blessed with the flowing white silk scarf that His Holiness had draped a few minutes earlier. I had crossed thousands who were jostling their way up to the institute, and had waved and nodded at me with knowing smiles. At the gate of the Institute, the director, faculty and other functionaries of the Tibetan Theatre Institute greeted me profusely, touching the ground in front of me, and thanking me with moist eyes, hands folded in Namaste. I could not comprehend why these thanks were coming even before the recital was performed. My escort, recognising my confusion, serenely explained that they were thankful to me for bringing His Holiness to the Institute for the first time, and that my visit to Dharamshala and giving a special dance programme was responsible for the Institute to be hallowed by the presence of His Holiness. My eyes brimmed over. Such intense love! Such unconditional devotion! Such deep faith! Each one in the crowd, each one at the Institute was a refugee, having left their beloved Tibet and all that they had possessed. They had faced untold hardships, humiliations and negativity before deciding to leave it behind and traverse the difficult Himalayan terrain to reach India, land of Gautama the Buddha. Yet their eyes shone with hope, and their smiles were wide, spontaneous and open. They unabashedly offered themselves to the rock of compassion and tolerance, the Dalai Lama.

With H.H. Dalai Lama and my musicians

After a two-hour performance, I was on the stage with my musicians to receive blessings from His Holiness. He came up, hugged me tight and asked in a choked voice, 'How did you know, Sabari is my Kula-Devi?' I was dumbfounded, awe-struck, and had goose bumps all over. Goddess Kula-Devi or God Kula-Devta is the presiding deity of the individual, the family, clan, tribe or the village.

At another time, I had danced on a specially placed platform in the Buddha Jayanti Park in Delhi when His Holiness consecrated the statue of Buddha before dedicating it to India. A week-long consecration ceremony on location was led by His Holiness himself, his deep sonorous voice reverberating. I had gone to do a recce earlier. As he saw me, he waved, nodded and gave me a conspiratorial smile. I was on cloud nine! I was in His space as it were. I had this feeling again in Gala-Vihar, Sri Lanka, when I was gazing at the supine Buddha in a Maha-parinirvaana moment. So, there I was—barely a teenage girl in a blue taffeta frock with faux pearl buttons and a black velvet sash, two thick braids folded up and tied with black velvet ribbons—smiling and staring at a young Dalai Lama in the mid1950s of the last century in Bombay. That was his first visit to India in the company of the then, Panchen-Lama. When His Holiness saw the photo before autographing it for me, his famous belly-laughter poured out. He repeatedly pointed at the girl in the photo and then at me and laughed some more. I was submerged in the Gangaa of his innocent mirth.

Chapter 22

A Glimpse of My Life as I See It Now

Being a woman is so beautiful. If I had not been a woman, I wouldn't have felt life so intensely. My growth as a woman and as an artist have gone hand in hand because I've grown through my experiences and the wisdom I've culled from them. But I've not yet reached that stage where I am able to assess myself. I would like to think I'm very beautiful. I would like to think I'm very frank and honest. But what are other people's feelings about me? I have been my best critic also. I'm short-tempered like my grandfather, which is nice because I'm able to forgive and forget and get it out of my system in five minutes flat. I don't harbour grudges. I owe it all to a very enlightened upbringing. You can't hide what you are. The sanskars imbibed in one's childhood give you direction and I'm really grateful for the sanskars my family gave me.

I was born in a Gujarati family in Bombay. My grandfather hailed from Surat, while my mother's family was from Saurashtra. She was brought up by her uncle, Amritlal Sheth, who was a judge during the Raj, and who later owned the popular daily newspaper, Janmabhoomi. My mother was very beautiful and fearless—taking part in the Independence movement, wielding the laathi with Mridula Sarabhai. She was in jail with Kasturba Gandhi, in the same cell. Even today, the Gurukul she started for girls among the Bhils of Gujarat, is one of the best. She lived till she was 103 and passed away in 2016. Till she was in her late eighties, she was absolutely fit. I bow my head to her.

My grandfather, Mangaldas Pakvasa, was a very well-known name. He would study under street lamps in Mumbai, and had topped the law exams. In those days, the papers were corrected in England. But after he came in contact with Gandhiji and Sardar Patel, he gave up his booming practice. That meant loss of earnings of Rs 30,000 a month! In those days, God knows what that would have meant! He was appointed one of the first five governors of free India in 1947. From 1947 to 1952, he was the Governor of the Central Provinces and Berar, which were later portioned into Madhya Pradesh and Maharashtra. From 1959 to 1962, he was the Governor of Mysore, later named Karnataka. He was also the Acting Governor of Undivided Bombay and again of Maharashtra.

My grandfather had given away everything to the nation, literally all his property in Surat, Khandala, and Bombay. Me, my parents and Dadaji lived in a rented apartment, and they didn't even have a car, because he had the courage of his convictions. I remember he told me that Lord Mountbatten was to visit Nagpur (then capital of CP & Berar) before leaving India and a list for all the requirements was sent from Delhi. My grandfather wrote back saying that he was a strict vegetarian and he did not serve alcohol, and asked if they could revise the menu. Lord Mountbatten showed the letter to Pandit Nehru who was very angry and asked my grandfather to send in his resignation. But when Panditji told Gandhiji about it, he said, 'What's wrong? Pakvasa is right'. When Mountbatten was told that my grandfather was sending in

Shri Mangaldas Pakvasa(Grandfather)

his resignation, he said, 'What nonsense! Of course not! If I don't eat meat or drink for three days, I'm not going to die. But I don't want to hurt anybody's feelings.'

My father was a very quiet person. He was a typical Surti (from Surat), whom one would describe as happy-go-lucky. He was simple in his habits and tastes, very humorous and quick-witted. These are the qualities a lot of people admire in me and they stem from his genes. He was in the cotton business, buying shares and multiplying them, but his real love was philately and he even won some prestigious international awards for the same.

My grandfather had a huge library, and I remember spending a lot of my time during vacations reading, going deeply into mythology. I know the Mahabharata quite well, even though, it's the Ramayana that usually everyone knows about. All kinds of people came to our house. I met Jain munis, Acharya Tulsi, Bohra chiefs, even Muslim qazis. Prince Aly Khan visited once. They were so taken up by my grandfather's charm that they came and visited him even when he was no longer the governor.

In Dadaji's Lap

It was a very Indian upbringing, yet very cosmopolitan and broad-based. Even chaprasis were addressed with respect and had to be called by names such as Chunni Lal ji; the suffix was an absolute must in the Raj Bhavans.

We are three siblings: my elder sister, my younger brother and myself. My sister and I were never made to feel that we were girls. We were educated in sports, dance, music and painting, so that one learned everything. I have very happy memories because I was given total freedom and all throughout, I studied in a co-educational school and college. I was in the Fellowship High-School in Bombay, a Gujarati medium school where the Quit India Movement protests had taken place. I am proud to say that I've played in those hallowed grounds. We also underwent military training at the Nasik Bhonsla Military School where Vasant Sathe was once a student. When I went home during the vacations, I used to attend the shivir (camp) for women run by my mother where I learnt riding, shooting, and took part in other such disciplines.

Several great names were our guests at the Raj Bhawans. These included M S Subbulakshmi, Bade Gulam Ali Khan, Bismillah Khan, Pandit Omkar Nath Thakur, Uday Shankar, Siddheshwari Devi, Hirabai Barodekar and other such revered names.

In our Bombay apartment we woke up to the sound of Bade Gulam Ali Khan's riyaaz, who lived across the street! At that time, Rukmini Devi was my ideal, Bala Saraswati was personified art and Shanta Rao, the epitome of majesty. These were the people I had seen and met in my childhood. In my Elphinstone college years, one would pop in to see exhibitions at the Jehangir Art Gallery in Bombay and discuss them with Dr Moti Chandra, the great scholar. I saw my first Kathakali performance in the company of K Bharaat Iyer, the great scholar whose book on this dance form is a landmark. Damyanti Joshi, the Jhaveri sisters and Sitara Devi were family friends. So, one grew up in the midst of all these great artistes.

My interest in dance was very obvious to everyone. Though both my sister Arti and I were learning, it was always I who was ready before the teacher would come, sort of bubbling to start. With music it was always 'aaj nahin kal, pet dukhta hai' and other such lame excuses, but the dance master said I had natural grace, a natural talent for dance. At that time we were in Bangalore, and my gurus were Prof U S Krishna Rao and his wife Chandrabhaga Devi, both wonderful people. I did my first fox-trot with my guru and also had my first gin-and-lime with him and his wife. They were so enlightened, and such a beautiful couple. He taught chemistry at Bangalore University, while Chandrabhaga Devi came from an eminent literary family.

Sonal

When my teachers decided it was time for my Arangetram, they intimated my parents. I had to go for classes twice a day. In our family, we informed the elders where we were going and what time we would be back. So, I went to my grandfather's office who was then Governor of Mysore and found him busy in a meeting with the then Chief Minister, Nijalingappa and B D Jatti, the Finance Minister. His secretaries were busy typing. I walked in there in my practice-saree and announced: 'Dadaji, I am going' in Gujarati. He just looked up and asked in Gujarati, 'Where are you going?' I said, 'For my dance class'. He said, 'But you went in the morning.' 'Then, he shouted, 'You're not going anywhere. Get back to your room!'

I asked, 'Why?'

He said, 'I won't have a dancer in my family.'

I was so hurt. So I went to the car, drove to the class and sobbed my heart out. They asked, 'What happened?' And, of course, the telephone started ringing, with calls from the Raj Bhavan. I sent back the car and it returned with a message, 'Bring her back'. I said, 'I'm not going back.' So my teachers called them up and said, 'We'll drop her home after the class.'

My grandfather didn't speak to me for three days after that. And I refused to speak to him and also refused to eat. It was a big tamasha. Finally, he gave in and said, 'Come, let's have a truce. Tell me.'

I said, 'You tell me. First, you teach me dance, and you encourage me and then? Why did you scold me in front of others? Then, you extol Rukmini Devi.' She was a great friend of his and referred to him as her boyfriend.

'And, on the other hand, you're saying all this'. Very sweetly, he explained, telling me that I should never use art as commerce or business. Today I know and understand what he meant.

Then he paid all expenses for my Arangetram!

My grandfather organised the Arangetram at the Raj Bhavan in June 1961. I was 17 then. The entire Cabinet, art-connoisseurs, and a number of dance teachers attended. Audience included the

Arangetram

Arangetram with Gurus and Musicians

Maharaja of Mysore. Devika Rani (the first lady of India's silver screen) and her Russian painter husband Svetoslav Roerich. Next day, I received a hand-written letter from this gracious lady. There was a beautiful pouch with silver engraving that she had sent a letter, along with a silver box of kumkum and fragrant golden champa flowers. She had written: 'You are a born dancer. You have it in you. Make this your yoga....'.

And she quoted to me what her German Guru Pabst had told her in Berlin: 'It is when you think you know that you don't know you really start learning'. I received so many gifts and letters, I took them all in my stride.

Those who had real talent went ahead, and those who didn't, sat at home after their arangetram! Simple! As for me people didn't even realise that I was the governor's grand-daughter. If he was asked, 'Is Sonal Pakvasa related to you?' he would say 'Oh, yes! she's my grand-daughter'. That was the end of it. Today, for ambitious parents, the arangetram is like a wedding, like the first step to Swarg. I always tell my students: 'You're just beginning to open the door and beyond that lies the whole vista.'

When I graduated in German Literature Honours from Elphinstone College, the question was, what would I do? Get married, go abroad on a scholarship or appear for the IAS? What made me say those four famous words— 'I want to dance', which brought everything to a standstill? My father, mother and grandfather, they all painted (in black) the consequences of wanting to pursue dance. I remember the scene. They said, you can do this or that and still dance. My grandfather said I had a lawyer's mind, so I should study law, while my father said, 'Perhaps, she can crack the competitive exam, join Foreign Service.'

On the other hand, I was being offered a scholarship to Germany. Naturally, they couldn't understand why I was chucking it all out. I said, 'No I don't want to do anything but dance.'

My family was very upset. Two days later I left home quietly for Bangalore, back to my Gurus. The word spread that Sonal has run away. Lots of rumours and social gossip followed but I was blissful in my Guru's home where I soaked in dance and music 24x7x365 till it was time to reconcile with my contrite family.

Sonal in uniform

By now Sonal Pakvasa was getting wide recognition as a promising Bharatanatyam dancer. I was accompanied by four wonderful musicians viz Anoor Suryanarayan (vocal and nattuvangam), Rangasami (mridangam) Chinappa (violin) and Doraisami (flute), all trained by my Gurus, who had encouraged them to guide me and look after me. I travelled to Mysore, Hubli, Dharwad, Gulbarga, Hospet, Mudhol, Jamkhandi, Badami, Shimoga, Mangalore, Udupi, Moodbidri, Dharmasthale, Mercara (Coorg) etc, dancing in the temples at Belur and Halebid. I was now invited to Hyderabad and Madras, Tanjore and Madurai. In Bombay, I danced for the inaugural festival of senior Dagar Brother's new School of Dhrupad. My recital was followed by Ustad Vilayat Khan (sitar). My presence was noted at various festivals by word of mouth, as my name travelled further up to Delhi. I danced at the International Film Festival inaugural ceremony to an audience comprising of Satyajit Ray, Akira Kurosawa and Andre Wajda! I also danced for the Lion's Club Charity. The first ever 3-day dance and music festival at Sapru House featuring stalwarts like Indrani Rehman, Damayanti Joshi, Roshan Kumari and Ustad Vilayat Khan had me dancing on the first day. Dr Charles Fabri described me as the new star of Bharatanatyam. He was the biggest name in arts journalism at that time. His reviews on dance and films in *The Statesman* decided future course of an artist or a film. *Hindustan Times*' ace photographer Kishore Parekh put my stage performance photo on front page. In short, I had made my mark in the elite circles of 1964 Delhi. I must mention the role of Indrani Rehman—the then reigning queen of dance in North India, in bringing me to Delhi. She had seen my regular class at my Guru's home in Bangalore from whom she had learnt some dances and was a regular visitor whenever in town. She recommended my name to Chetan Garg, the influential Manager of Sapru House who was going to organise the first ever dance and music festival. Sapru House stage was much coveted, vying with AIFACS. Alas, now both are nearly defunct. Garg invited me for the opening performance and the rest is history.

Many things happened during this visit to Delhi: an argument with family friend and the then Finance Minister Shri Morarji Desai where I was staying, some classes with Smt. Swarna Saraswati to learn padams; getting introduced in the intellectual art circles and the warmth of being hosted and toasted by many of the celebrities of the time. I was innocent to the effect I had on others which carries on till now, a quality inherited from my wonderful Dadaji. Nothing was as important as dance. Nothing was more attractive than to learn and absorb. I met painters, sculptors, musicians and poets of Delhi. That visit may have been one of the turning points in my life.

There was a phase when there was a desire for more and more programmes and one didn't look beyond that. Having performed all over the Asian subcontinent, in Europe, and in the deep interiors of India, I now find that a recital is not the be-all and end-all of life. This has come out of the process of growing inwards. If tomorrow, people say they don't want to see me anymore, I'm not going to turn upside down, do two or three tumbles and say, 'My God. My life is finished!' Dance has been a very enriching experience, but life is so much greater.

Dance has been one constant flame in my life. I never lost sight of it and I am used to being centre-stage. That does not mean that I am a narcissist. It means that I am at the centre-stage of my own life. I live life consciously but with dignity. That's the true meaning of life for me.

Chapter 23

Kiradu

The Perfect Beauty

I have felt, tasted, heard, and seen. I have experienced a plethora of things: cow-bells; the morning breeze and pink sky at dawn; stark hills; silhouettes; pillars carved like jewels and figures smiling with serenity—destroyed, yet indestructible. I have experienced beauty so complete, so full that one had to close their eyes to shut off the actual, physical vision and replay only the inner vision, the total experience being something akin to Ananda, complete Bliss.

The symmetry or the proportion, of the carved voluptuousness or the easy fluidity, the rounded bosoms and hips, the curve of the smiling lips and arch of the amorous eyebrows, the tilt of the long gaze, dangling pom-poms and swaying scarves, arms slender as creepers upraised to entwine, embrace, beckon, hold the child, decorate the hair or simply for the pleasure of feeling one's own body alive and pulsating. Boulders hiding serpents. Dust covering stones with horses, elephants, Yakshas, Apsaras, verily, ashes to ashes, dust to dust, stone meeting stone.

Beauty stark and primeval merging back into contemplated beauty. Creation so underlined with activity and repose, like

Kiradu temple

music with perfectly melodious lines, music of lilting pauses, like the pillars only half-carved, sudden glides to jolt the senses back to the reality of this creation. Spirit soaring up and up like the blue sky, the only witness to the phenomenon of Samadhi. I understand the truth of Ananda on the face of a living dancer as on the faces of those in stones, paintings or wood carvings—a smile perched lightly like a precious butterfly ready to take off at the first hint of some inner disturbance or turbulence, yet radiating joy and warmth.

That strict adherence to the norms and rules of Shilpa Shastra (science of architecture, iconography, and idol-making) can lead mortals to the path of Divinity was well known. We also learned to follow the classical discipline of dancing to the perfect tala, laya, and rasa and thus make a votive offering at the temple of Kalaa, the Arts. Art alone can move the human soul, which otherwise is given too much to reasoning and demanding logical explanations for unknown ecstacies. Knowing that art alone can produce a melody so subtle, so divine that only with the inner ear one can relish its sweetness. After my car accident this was the decisive experience and tears rolled down my cheek. But these were welcome tears of uncontrollable, inexpressible joy. It is a bliss so total that one can become speechless. Is this a glimpse of the mystery of Creation?

Very close to Indo-Pak border Kiradu is situated near Badmer in Rajasthan, a cluster of stone temples now in ruins. When I

Kiradu temple-4-1

The Kiradu Temples in perspective

wrote this in my diary in 1978 there was no evidence of Archaeological Servey of India's presence there except a routine notice. A local elder made rounds trying to stop routine pilferage by villagers and occasional visitor. Even today Kiradu is hardly known perhaps because of the location or apathy of 'progress' oriented generations.

Chapter 24

Maryaada

No, this is not the name of a Hindi masala film. This is a word in Sanskrit which defines a certain aspect of Indian culture. Once, after my regular morning rehearsal, I called a person aside to ask about the remuneration. He had been giving me rigorous classes in Odissi. We had started work three weeks ago without going into such mundane details. But now the moment had come since I was leaving on a dance tour within a day. His reply stunned me. With folded hands, he begged me to desist from making such inquiries. I pressed him, saying that I did not know about what was expected. With a hurt expression, he said that working with me had been a great joy and a lesson for him, and that he never asks any fees from even his usual disciples either and accepts whatever is given as God's gift.

Here was the very concept of maryaada, the respect inherent in relationships, the mutual regard and understanding, the setting up of self-imposed limits, not limitations.

A well-known saying is that 'When ocean gives up, it's maryaada, who can save the world'. Even in nature, the elements must maintain their balance. Seasons must follow each other as

Bhrigu-Rishi

ordained, bringing beauty and harmony in creation. In the animal world, a respectful distance is maintained at all times between competing males. Their harems keep a vigilant distance from both. The moment one of them breaks the code, fierce battle ensues. The code of conduct also includes the concept of maryaada.

In India, this has been an integral part of our thinking. Attitudes and behavioural patterns have been shaped in accordance with certain norms which have synthesised centuries of influences and cross-cultural polarities. The inner landscape of India has remained largely unchanged despite millenia of checkered history.

One of the many apocryphal stories on this subject is also one of my favourite. Sage Bhrigu decided to test the true greatness of each of the Trinity–Brahma, Vishnu and Mahesh. He boldly walked into their respective abodes and kicked the divine beings on the chest. Brahma warned of impending thunder. Shiva threatened to open His Third Eye to burn him. Vishnu caught hold of the offending foot, massaged it and was sorry that his hard chest might have hurt the delicate foot of the sage. Can we understand the meaning and symbolism of each of these actions? Was it not to impart patience and insight into our daily behaviour, actions and reactions? This is what we learn in India, specially through the Guru-shishya relationship. The maryaada inherent in touching the Guru's feet, bowing the head and accepting the Guru as the potter who will mould one into shape is an interesting concept. Having learnt to dance through this system, I recognise the merits and recommend it strongly. The Guru's interest in the pupil's wellbeing and progress is deep. The pupil responds by

Gurus

My revered Gurus

placing faith and trust in the Guru by following instruction and showing respect in matters, both big and small. Contrary to popular belief, this does not preclude an animated or well-argued discussion on the merits and demerits of certain postures or interpretations or designs of a costume. This is the truly classical concept which is applicable to other relationships as well. The give-and-take between parents and children, the mutual regard between husband and wife and the affectionate understanding between friends—appreciating the strong points but not overlooking the weak ones, rather endeavouring to make the other aware of them to help overcome those issues.

In each of these, the limit beyond which one should be cautious is to be understood. Even in the strongest of relationships there are areas which are best left untouched. We all require our own time and space, not just physical but emotional, and which with time becomes a spiritual need. To have an area of retreat within oneself is very important. Yoga, sadhana, and meditation are all forms of creating this inner space.

The outer or Bahya expressions of this inner space is maryaada. It is the vibrant, palpitating distance—in the case of dance between the dancer and the musicians; dancer and her audience; and dancer and the dance. The profound respect and regard one has for the other is manifested in the level of magnanimity, generosity and largeness of the heart. This is where one dancer speaks well about the other, a critic or Rasika speaks appreciatively of a dancer who has lived, breathed and given herself fully to dance. It is then that the level of a civilisation is gauged, the true essence of a culture measured, when those who manage art also have a profound knowledge and respect for the art and artist, for the younger and for the established ones, the inexperienced or the mature. Without observing maryaada in speech, action and thought we might be extolling just the empty shell of our 'culture'. Let that day not come to pass.

Chapter 25

My Jagannath

In 1965, I met Shri Jagannath formally. My would-be father-in-law, Dr Mayadhar Mansingh, took me to Puri during my fortnight of getting-to-know the family ritual, following the engagement ceremony in Cuttack, Odisha. In the absence of the groom, I was betrothed to an ancient sword. As I was already a known name in Bharatanatyam, Dr Mansingh insisted that I learn Odissi. My Odissi lessons began with him taking me to the Kala-Vikash-Kendra in Cuttack where a group of functionaries waited to receive us. Among them were late Shri Babulal Doshi, the founder-president and late Guru Kelucharan Mahapatra. Bapa simply said (in Oriya of course) 'Kelu! This is Sonal, my daughter-in-law. You will teach her Odissi'.

For the weekend, he took me on a trip to Shri Jagannath Puri, something I had looked forward to ever since I began to learn dance. As Chidambaram Nataraja was to Bharatanatyam, Jagannath at Puri is for Odissi; this much I had gathered from my reading and watching Indrani Rehman's first programme in Bombay in which she had included two items from the Odissi repertory. For those two items, the Jagannath idol was ensconced

Jagannatha Puri

on stage in the corner opposite to where the musicians sat. That suddenly seemed to become the centre of attraction for the audience as, so far, Bombay had only seen Nataraja in Bharatanatyam recitals. I too peered at Him and loved the wide, knowing grin and huge painted eyes as round as the globe!

I stood in the sanctum sanctorum in front of the Ratna-Vedi in the temple at Puri, abode of the Lord of the Universe. I knew that He was not alone, but my eyes were unprepared for the majesty of the three gorgeous figures staring at me. I had to close my eyes, then look, close my eyes again, and finally look until I could stare back. Then that Netra-Milan happened—that electric moment of recognition, of an unbroken chain of births and lives. Jagannath's smile seemed to broaden, the round huge eyes—Chaka Dola—full of mirth and mischief as if saying 'So, you have come, haan?'

Bapa woke me from that trance with his usual merry laugh. Aarti was prepared, and I watched with folded hands and a heart full of wonderment; is this a dream? Blessed Subhadra looked petite and friendly, whereas the elder brother Balabhadra was imposing. Sudarshana Chakra completed the Chaturdha Moorti somewhat like Shri Hanuman with Shri Ram, Sita and Lakshman. I remember even sitting down in front of the Ratna-Vedi and singing "Pralaya Payodhi Jale" the entire Dasavatara from the Geeta-Govinda of Kavi Jayadeva, but in Carnatic style to which I had danced in Bharatanatyam.

I have carried that effulgent presence inside me since that day. Over the years, I have had many darshans, many occasions to chat with my Jagannath with the benign form of Subhadra looking on. Balabhadra stares directly in front, no deviations for him, unlike the younger brother!

People have reported a presence on stage, dancing with me, through the Ashtapadis of Geeta-Govinda. I have felt the touch, the breath, the tears of bliss running down the cheeks unsummoned, undeterred. His outstretched arms can encompass millions of solar systems, then why not me?

Jagannatha Temple Puri Odisha

I have, at a crucial moment in 1972, stood before him in my two-room apartment in Delhi full of rage and fury. I have scolded, shouted, and demanded an explanation. I remember ending my tirade by warning Him: 'From now on, everything happening to me, everything I do, good or bad goes to you. I shall carry no burden.'

I have begun to see clearer images of this Divyataa—the presence which seems to expand and contract according to my moods. I feel that He might be getting bored with so much adulation, kowtowing, demands, and prayers. I must make Him laugh. So, my self-appointed title is 'The Clown of Jagannath!' We share jokes, incidents, funny situations, even with Subhadra listening in. Balabhadra remains indifferent as usual. When I danced Shriya Chandalini, He was there guiding my steps towards the Golden Palace of Sri Lakshmi. He came behind me, hiding in my shadow to get a glimpse of his beloved consort Lakshmi. I was blessed. Oh, how and why should one open up the entire treasure of one's relationship with Him? Let something remain unsaid.

Shri Jagannath Vijayate! Victory to Him, Master of the Universe.

Chapter 26

Ramayana as Narrated in Ramcharit Manas by Tulsidaas

The sixteenth century in the northern Indian context was predominantly Islamic, when Akbar ruled from Agra and his empire held sway over most of North India, stretching well into Afghanistan. Tulasidas lived in a society engaged with a strange amalgam of old Hindu culture and tradition now increasingly being informed by Muslim thinking and attitudes. Tulasidaas wrote his Ramayana-*Ramcharit Manas* on the banks of the river Gangaa in the holy city of Varanasi. The place is still revered by devotees and scholars alike and is known as Tulsi Ghat. There is a small shrine where remains of his boat which ferried him to the middle of the river for a bath is worshipped.

For those familiar with the Valmiki Ramayana, the version penned by Tulasi will show many differences. Sage Valmiki was a contemporary of Prabhu Shri Rama. His Ramayana containing 24000 verses in Sanskrit is divided into Seven 'Kaand' or Canto, 'Adhyaya'. This epic poem is accurate report of Shri Rama's life and deeds, presenting a different perspective from the latter day versions like *Ramcharit Manas* and *Kamba Ramayana* among others. Valmiki's Sita is a tejaswini, a woman of substance who speaks her mind, questions Rama openly about many of his actions. Tulasi's Sita is from a milieu which existed in sixteenth century North India when women were increasingly confined to home and hearth. A general perception about the need for women to be heard, but not seen, had taken root. Male-oriented values were in vogue. Many such traits are seen in Tulasi's narrative.

Valmiki saw Rama as a Man but for Tulasi he is Superman, God in the form of a human who could do no wrong and whose actions or motives were beyond question. Yet for our times, especially in the Hindi-speaking belt of North India, Tulasi's version has found an enduring place in the hearts and minds of the people. While dealing with episodes from the *Valmiki Ramayana,* Tulasi has taken some liberties as is natural and imbued the story with his own perceptions and understanding. Indeed, this is one of the greatest examples of intellectual liberty allowing freedom of thought and action.

Katha Siya-Ram ki: Marriage of Sita

In the Sita-Swayamvara episode I had selected for my performance in the 2008 Natya Kala Conference at Chennai, even though the flow of the narrative touches upon every vital point, the poetry remains very much that of Tulasi. The Avadhi language has its own cadences, sound and imagery which gives the narrative a decisively local flavour. The now popular tune of the Doha and Chaupai of Manas have gained wide acceptance even in other parts of India.

Tulasi frequently uses utpreksha and atishayokti (exaggeration) alankaras to enhance his narrative when he describes the disappointment of thousands of emperors and kings assembled to win Sita's hand. None succeed even in lifting the mighty bow

सियावररामचन्द्र की जय
Victory to Ramchandra, the husband of Sita

स्वयंवर की जयमाला
Offering wedding garland

of Shiva. Tulasi gives a comic flavour by saying that after losing their reputation and lustre, the kings decide to join hands, to lift the bow and thus 10,000 of them came together to lift the bow. And yet, they are unable to move that mighty bow Pinak, given by God Shiva to king Janak, even by an inch. The description of Lakshman's furious repartee to King Janak who laments the absence of a single hero on earth who can perform the task was being narrated in the story-line. I was to dance it at Varanasi's Banaras Hindu University's golden jubilee celebrations in the late 1970s, when suddenly a young man stood up from the audience, pulling at his moustache, and roared 'Aawat hain'—'I am coming!' So engrossed was he that in his mind the place and occasion had blurred, taking him back to that moment of King Janak's disappointment.

There was stunned silence and then a wave of laughter as everyone realised how involved the young man had become in the narrative! At the end of the episode, as I danced the departure of Sita with Rama for Ayodhya, I could feel the sobbing, teary-eyed women in the audience.

The story of Rama and Sita still arouses our tender sentiments, reduces us to tears holding out a huge promise of a continuing stream of elevated consciousness which flows within us as the timeless Gangaa. May all the Ramayana ever written, sung, danced to, woven, sculpted or painted give us our daily Redemption!

Chapter 27

Transforming Society

The Role of Women

In India, and indeed in many parts of our world where ancient civilisations flourished and also among the tribal societies, woman as Mother received the highest honour. In India, the four-fold salutations place mother at the top:

Maatru Devo Bhava-Mother is God (divine)

Pitrudevo Bhava-Father is God

Gurudevo bhava-Teacher is God

Atithidevo bhava-Guest is God (literally 'the unannounced guest')

'A mother is equal to a hundred teachers' goes another proverb. The miracle of nature happens within the mother's womb. New life takes shape, breathes, is nourished and cherished in the mother's body by partaking of her flesh and blood. She sows seeds of goodness and honesty early in life. She teaches values which guide us on the right path.

The female of the species are entrusted with the task of regeneration and perpetuation which essentially is a reflection of Prakriti, the all-absorbing nature of Creation. Nature keeps the process and systems going by which Creation is sustained.

Therefore, a woman in India has been equated to Devi (the Great Goddess) who in different manifestations fulfills every important role imaginable.

A woman is needed in every field of activity. Her support, guidance and wisdom steer a family through thick and thin. Her tenacity and emotional stamina are the rudder of the ship called Life. India, with its diversity and divisions in society based on religion, caste, language, and other factors such as economic strata defies sweeping generalisations. Yet, to comprehend the positive role of women in society, one has to keep in mind a few points like the divide between rich and poor, rural and urban etc which are now hackneyed phrases, so are categories of women as householders, skilled or unskilled workers, entrepreneurs, teachers, lawyers, doctors, politicians, bureaucrats.

In Independent India, many new avenues and fields have opened to accept and promote women. Here I would like to narrow down the vast canvas to the area of the arts, by which I mean performing and visual arts. Here is where women have been at once wanted and shunned, feared and worshipped. Women dancers and musicians were an essential part of society, and were the ones to perform rituals in temples, to entertain and also instruct the royal courts and noble households, tutor their young in the art of living. Sculptures and paintings from temples and rock-cut caves like Ellora, Barhut, and Khandagiri, and frescoes and murals of Ajanta bear witness to the importance and significance of the performing arts in society. In the era of Janapadas and Ganarajyas (city-states) like the Lichhavis and in erstwhile Kalinga, Raja-nartaki (dancer in the royal court) enjoyed equal status as the chieftain-king and the raj-guru (royal preceptor) in her right to use the royal umbrella and chariot! From an assured respected position, the female dancer became a poor reflection of the past glory due to centuries of attacks, resulting in political upheavals, economic deprivation and social degradation.

Her role throughout India, indeed the pan-Indian image, suffered a severe setback, so much so that just before their final departure from India, the British enacted Devadasi Act banning all dancing in temples. Certain so-called Indian reformists joined hands in perpetuating the unjust and derogatory insult alleging that Devadasis were prostitutes and therefore were to be ousted from respectable places of worship, indeed from entire civil society!

This mentality has a direct link to my story of becoming a dancer. Remember the anecdote of 1961 I recounted when my paternal grandfather Shri Mangaldas Pakvasa was Governor of Mysore, and had instructed me sternly not to go to meet my Bharatanatyam Gurus Prof and Smt U S Krishna Rao? But I had defied him and snuck out. My grandfather was so annoyed that

The Arangetram: 6th June 1961, Bangalore

he had not spoken to me for three (3) days. I did not speak to him either and had not eaten for three (3) whole days, remember, I was a young dancer and always hungry!

Then Grandpa also refused to eat and this action on his part, forced me to relent. Later he apologised to me. He also explained about his apprehensions, that is when I first learned of the black mark against dancing-girls and their social ostracisation.

Yet dancers have found a firm place in India's history. Not only Devadasis, but queens like Santala and saintly women like Lalded, Meera and Mahadevi Akka danced in ecstasy. My own dancing has given me deep insights into the raison d'etre of the abiding and continuing popularity of dance in India.

Through dance, women professed their love for gods, beauty and the flow of life. Various social ills and shortcomings of people could be pointed out in a manner that was immediate and attractive without being sanctimonious or judgmental. Issues of ecology and environment, cruelty and violence, inequality and inadequacy, indeed issues of everyday life or larger than life could be tackled and spoken about in an artistic manner which established direct connection with people.

My own experiences of such happenings are numerous. My solo dance-theatre Draupadi not only made the 300 members of Parliament numb and tearful but also remorseful which they later confessed to the Speaker, Shivraj Patil. Some of them swore to take up women's problems like rape, torture, and molestation in their constituencies, and sincerely work at getting them justice. My portrayal of children at play being protected from dangerous situations against all odds by Mother, delineating episodes of Savitri, Madaalasaa's lullaby for baby son, Ahilyabais life and deeds—the list is unending, names which inspire us even today.

In short, raising consciousness and the conscience through

Draupadi

the arts, retelling stories, songs, and parables which essentially belong to the realm in which a woman plays her role as the pillar of the family and backbone of the social structure, is what brings about social transformation. Through subtle yet strong means, a woman is able to alter rigid mindsets, fight against unhealthy practices, eradicate social evils like alcoholism, criminality and other vices. Woman-power in many villages has manifested in unusual ways. They have collectively been able to withdraw sexual favours to their husbands who were thus forced to give up their vicious indulgences. Without Shakti, even Shiva becomes a Shava, a corpse. What can one say about ordinary mortals then? Let women guide the course of future transformations to establish the rule of 'Satyam, Shivam, Sundaram' (Truth, Beauty, Auspiciousness).

Chapter 28

Woman

Ancients spoke not only about divinity of Creation but also of woman, emphasising the respect she deserves, because by worshipping her, the Gods are pleased. Therefore, one must worship, love, respect and cherish her! I always extend my best wishes to all the men in India and the world on occasions like International Women's Day on 8 March, although I do so with a few quotes to tease men out of their smug stupor. 'I am extraordinarily patient provided I get my own way in the end,' said Margaret Thatcher, erstwhile British PM. 'The male ego with few exceptions is elephantine to start with,' said Mae West, Hollywood actress known for her chutzpah. 'He was the cock who thought the Sun had risen to hear him crow!' said woman author George Eliot back in the 1800s.

The credit for getting 8 March designated as International Women's Day goes to two German women, Luise Zietz and Clara Zetkin. One wonders why in earlier centuries women were not allotted even one day of reverence; perhaps, because they were to be loved and cared for throughout life. So now has the time come to designate an International Day of Men too?

Indian dance celebrates women as perhaps no other art form does. The physical and emotional sensibilities of the female are in full display in Indian dance forms. They are celebrated for bringing change, opening up new paths, infusing passion, love and beauty in daily life. The ability of a woman to shape new life and create something extraordinary from the ordinary is truly awe-inspiring. Throughout history, women have reinvented paradigms for dignity, equality and freedom. Although the history of the world is written by men, women's history of the world dominates the script. Otherwise, from where would men have appeared? Her womb is

Inanna-Sumerian-God- Annunaki

the womb of Creation from which men and women come forth—men such as Rama and Krishna, Buddha and Mahaveer, Christ Nanak, Vikramaditya, Rajendra Chola—great or ordinary woman is Mother to all. She is the representative of Prakriti, the mysterious nature. She is Mahamaya, the great conspirator. She is Shakti, the power behind Creation. Indian dance deals with the absolutely mundane to supra-mundane concept of Woman in a superbly convincing manner.

I have been amazed and overwhelmed by women's history in India. Many of my own choreographies are pegged on women such as Raadha, Draupadi, Ahalya, Meera, Lalded, Kasturba Gandhi, Bhikaiji Cama, and others amongst a galaxy of luminous women. It is noteworthy how each one is fearless and brooks no indignity. Such women have written and lived life according to

Pancha Kanyaa

Mandala

their own script and idea of womanhood. I have paid my homage in dance to succeeding generations of self-confident, brilliant, strong yet compassionate women whose lives are a message for contemporary times as well.

Indic family traditions teach us to respect four entities. The first is the mother, 'Matru Devo Bhava, Mother is God'. The next are Father, Guru and Guest! I have celebrated woman as mother in my works such as Jabaalaa, who honestly and fearlessly told the great Rishi Gautam that as she had served many masters hence did not know who her son Satyakaam's father was. All she knew as the truth was that she was Jabaalaa, the mother and Satyakaam was her son. The Rishi rose from his seat to offer respect to this Satyavaadini, speaker of truth. Her son, Satyakaam, grew up to become one of the greatest Rishis in Upanishadic times. As I showed Jabalaa washing clothes in the Narmadaa River and drying them under the sun, I could visualise this most ordinary woman with extraordinary strength of character.

I triumphed in questioning the orthodox concept of considering Krishna as Paramaatma—Supreme Self—and Raadha as Jeevaatma—Individual Self—constantly yearning to unite. My Raadha is different; independent, dignified and one with her own super-conscious Self. Similarly, my interpretation of the legendary Pancha-Kanyaa—Ahalyaa, Taaraa, Kunti, Draupadi and Mandodari—aroused great interest and debate in various quarters. As I have believed in research, thought and action, I always welcome questions, doubts and debates because 'Woman' is the ultimate mystery and not enough has been said about her.

Devi

'Aaj ki kanyaa' asks men to be considerate, respectful, humble, thoughtful and loving. I wonder if that is too much to ask? A rose and lotus are both beautiful and fragrant. The rose is surrounded by thorns, while the lotus rises out of mud. Both have different identity and character. Both fight odds and obstacles, and yet triumph. Being in our own skin, with our own identities and attributes, both can and should be like two wheels of a chariot, like two eyes creating one vision.

The story of the human race, you will agree, begins with Woman!

Praise for the Book

When a multi-dimensional personality like Dr Sonal Mansingh, who is not merely an individual or an artist, but a living institution in herself and embodies the very best, most sublime and pristine elements of Bharatiya Sanskriti, comes up with a compilation of articles written at various stages of her illustrious and eventful life, one naturally sits up and takes notice. At first glance, the articles in this book might appear disconnected or as the title says the output of *A ZigZag Mind*. But on closer contemplation and reading, one realises that they are the distillate and sum-total of the intense sadhana that this artist has undertaken in the last seven decades or so. They are not merely flippant stories related just to her life and experiences; but have become windows to understanding the quintessence of Bharatiya civilisation, philosophy and art—all of which Sonal ji has not merely written about or spoken from a pulpit in a scholarly manner; but through her own lived experiences, breathed life and her uniqueness to them, thereby enriching the culture of this great land. In the pages of this book, one therefore finds the sacrifice, the lived experience, the accrued wisdom and the universal knowledge that an artist par excellence like her has burnished through the intense fire of sadhana. It therefore transcends immediately from the mere personal to the universal in a manner that is impossible if one is not soaked deeply in the art and its philosophy. For instance, the intertwining of the story of the seven rivers or 'Sapta-nadi' with their spiritual significance, the Pauranic tales and folk-lore associated with them, the art-forms that flourished on their banks and in short, they becoming the very warp and weft of Bharatiya Sanskriti is not something that can be brought out through uni-dimensional scholarship. It is only when a sadhaka like Sonal ji alchemises these seemingly disparate threads into one cogent mix that the larger picture emerges clearer than one ever imagined. The book is replete with numerous such revelations on Raadha, Krishna, Vishnu, Shiva, Devi, Rama and what they mean to the essence of Bharat. In a touching personal anecdote, Sonal ji's resilience and never-say-die attitude in the wake of life-threatening experiences and nadirs leaves a reader teary-eyed, but also charged with inspiration and admiration for her chutzpah. Far from being the output of a zig-zag mind, the book is a conglomerate of essential reading for anybody who wishes to known about the soul of Bharat—one that has been eluding sages, savants and seekers for centuries; making itself visible in glimpses through our art-forms, literature and philosophy. Elegantly-written, richly-referenced and beautifully illustrated, this latest offering from Sonal ji is a pleasure to read and a collector's delight!

Dr Vikram Sampath, FRHistS
Author, Historian, Fellow of the
Royal Historical Society, UK

The enduring mystique of Dr Sonal Mansingh's five decades of performative brilliance unfolds in the book she has compiled called *A ZigZag Mind.* Here is the story of inspiration and struggle, opportunities and losses, and, most of all, the triumph of passion for dancing. Looking at Sonal's dazzling presence and mesmerising programmes, one may come away thinking this is a charmed life. But the book tracks the sheer grit and hard decisions that made Sonal who she is—an unparalleled dancer, a choreographer, scholar and innovator with a deep commitment to Indian traditions.

Prof Malashri Lal
Academic and Creative Writer, Convener,
English Advisory Board, Sahitya Akademi

What can one say about Dr Sonal Mansingh ji that has not already been said. She is India's greatest living classical dancer. There can be no doubt in that. Many of us have had the privilege of seeing her dance, and it wouldn't be hyperbole to say that we come away changed after the experience. But even more subtle than Dr Sonal ji's dance, is her insightful mind. Steeped in ancient Indian traditions, trained in modern ways, and with the blessings of the Mother Goddess, Dr Sonal ji's astute takes on India and its culture, will help us understand this great land that much more deeply. Read this book not just to appreciate Dr Sonal ji's brilliant mind, but also Indian culture at its finest.

Amish Tripathi
Author

Dr Sonal Mansingh's book *A ZigZag Mind* is truly inspiring. A dancer and scholar par excellence, this book brings out not only her knowledge in various aspects of life in abundance, but also her experience and approach to life in an educative manner which is truly amazing.

Subhalakshmi Khan
Indian Dancer

A ZigZag Mind by Dr Sonal Mansingh gives such a remarkable perspective to the journey called life. A must read for all!'

Ustad Amjad Ali Khan
Sarod Maestro

Sonal Mansingh wears her immense erudition and wisdom in the field of the classical arts very lightly. She writes with passion, precision, and conviction. This is an immensely readable book with varied reflections on classical dance, Indian performing arts, aesthetics, culture and civilisation. She also includes several riveting chapters recalling the horrific injuries she received in a car accident in 1974 and the sheer grit and determination that helped effect a miraculous recovery that took her back to the dance stage again in less than a year. These make for riveting and inspirational reading, as, indeed, does her take on each subject her zig zag mind chooses to touch upon.

Sunit Tandon
Media and Theatre Personality

A ZigZag Mind is a fantastic collection of articles written on a diverse array of related subjects by one of Bharat's finest dance exponents. The articles showcase not only Dr Sonal Mansingh's command over her art form, but serve to capture her deep understanding of Bharat's sanatani traditions that undergird the art. That there is a full-fledged writer in her waiting to be tapped into is evident from this collection of her thoughts. One hopes that she will write more, especially on the deep and inextricable relationship between bhakti, sanskriti and kala at a time when one sees a motivated and accelerated push towards secularisation of our arts to enable its misappropriation.

J Sai Deepak

Advocate, Supreme Court of India and Author

These rambling notes, *A ZigZag Mind*, express a unified creativity that weaves a brahmaleena yogi, a dancer, a river and a woman into the same continuum of a 'chaosmos' of passionate desire, restless movement, and symphony of meanings, music, movement and the final accomplished moment of spiritual stasis. So when Sonal ji dances, the dancer, dancing and the dance become one, releasing the sa-hrdaya from his small self and making him one with the divine.

Kapil Kapoor

Former Professor of English &

Concurrent Professor of Sanskrit Studies

JNU New Delhi

[illegible]

[illegible]

[illegible]

Kapil Kapoor

Former Professor [illegible]

[illegible]

JNU, New Delhi